Yaquina Lighthouses

Aerial views: Yaquina Head Lighthouse (top)
Yaquina Bay Lighthouse (lower)

Yaquina

Lighthouses

On The Oregon Coast

Dorothy Wall
(With Bert Webber)

Webb Research Group Publishers

Published by
Webb Research Group
P. O. Box 314
Medford, Oregon 97501

<u>**Library of Congress Cataloging In Publications Data:**</u>
Wall, Dorothy, 1926-
    Yaquina Lighthouses on the Oregon Coast / Dorothy Wall with
Bert Webber.
        p.   cm.
    Includes bibliographical references and index.
        ISBN 0-936738-07-3
        1. Lighthouses – Oregon– Yaquina Bay – History. [2. Lighthouses
    – Oregon – Yaquina Head – History] I. Webber, Bert. II. Title.
VK1024.07W35   1993   93-26330
387.1'55 – dc20   [Published 1994]   CIP

<u>**For catalogers seeking alternate or additional subject headings:**</u>
Try: 614.8 – Accidents - prevention \ safety through regulation –
                    protective measures
            623.8 – Navigation
For catalogers recognizing ghost story classifications:
Try: 808.83'72 – Mystery – suspense
            398.47 – Folklore – unreal – ghosts
            398.323 – Folklore – haunted places

Contents

Historic sign for historic lighthouse as viewed about 1973.

Introduction

Yaquina Bay Lighthouse was built in the area where Captain James Cook made his first landfall along the Pacific Coast of what became America. This was on March 7, 1778.

This lighthouse on the bluff overlooking the entrance to the bay was primarily a harbor-entrance light and was equipped with a 5th Order lens. Under no fog and with clear-air conditions, it was visible 11 miles.

It can also be said that Yaquina *Head* Lighthouse was built in the same area where Captain James Cook made his first landfall because the two locations are only a few miles apart. As we shall see, the English captain was looking at the land from his ship some distance at sea.

Yaquina Head Lighthouse, about 3½ miles north of Yaquina Bay Lighthouse, was needed as a warning for the rocky 60-feet high headland that protruded well into the ocean. A ship whose skipper was not familiar with the area running near the shore at night bound for the entrance to Yaquina Bay and following that light, could run into this headland not knowing it was there. The Yaquina Head Lighthouse operated with a 1st Order lens with a visibility in good weather of 19 miles.

When the larger lighthouse was completed, the smaller was discontinued.

Probably every lighthouse that ever existed is the seat of ghost stories and the lights here are certainly no different. When the Federal Writer's Project was created during the Great Depression years, the guide book *Oregon, End of the Trail,* that finally appeared in 1940, on page 376, declares:

Newport has a HAUNTED LIGHTHOUSE

Almost immediately, people started flocking to the lighthouse to "check it out." They keep coming even to the present day! Are there really ghosts in these two lighthouses? We'll see.

*   *   *

I first wish to thank to Rick Taylor, Oregon State Parks, for

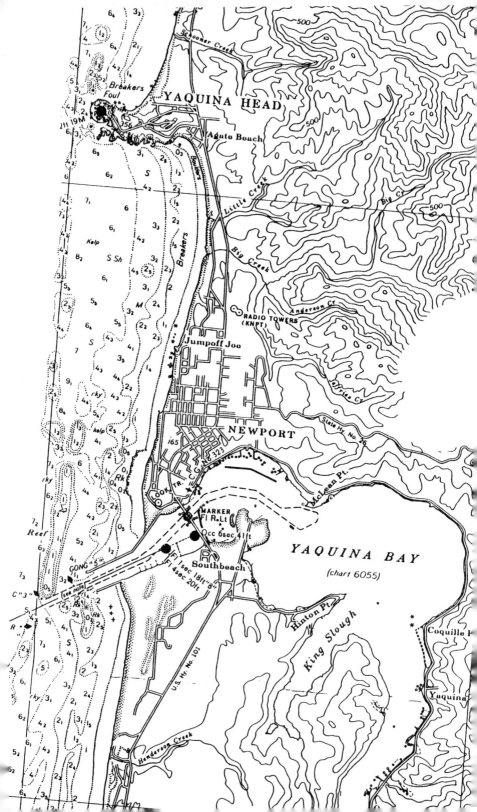

choosing me and my husband to host at the lighthouse.

My heartfelt thanks to Elizabeth Walton Potter, Oregon State Parks, for information about the restoration of the lighthouse.

I am indebted to Jim Gibbs, author of many books about Oregon Coast lighthouses and shipwrecks, who always finds time to help me with my questions.

To Ken Black, Curator of Maine's Lighthouse Museum, the Shore Village Museum, Rockland, Maine, a special thank you for his friendly encouragement and guidance through the technical maze dealing with the uniqueness and differences between the various Fresnel lenses.

I gladly remember Wayne Wheeler of the U. S. Lighthouse Society, San Francisco, for his willingness to discuss some of the details about the lenses.

Don Giles, Newport, Oregon, took us on the nature walk a-round the lighthouse reservation and made us more aware of the plants that we had taken for granted. His knowledge, interest and enthusiasm all played a valuable part in forming this book and I thank him.

We appreciate the help of the descendants of the Peirce family who shared family records. These were Bob McClain, Terri Shelby, Agnes Daniels and John Goodman.

A writing project such as this one takes a lot of time and encouragement especially when I bogged down. First, my husband, Les, has always been an encourager and I publicly thank him here. There was also Mike Rivers and Monte Turner, Oregon State Parks Department, who often helped with the right words.

I was pleased when Bert Webber, publisher of Webb Research Group, read the unfinished manuscript and agreed to work with me to develop this book. There were many others who helped from time to time and I want to thank them all.

There may be further data about the lighthouse, as well as anecdotes, about which I am unaware. Readers who wish to share additional information may reach me in care of the publisher whose address is on page iv.

Dorothy Wall
Yaquina Bay Lighthouse
Winter 1993-1994

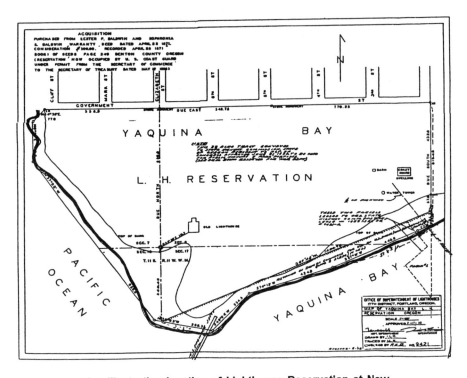

Map illustrating location of Lighthouse Reservation at Newport, Oregon. The property is bounded by the Pacific Ocean in the westerly direction, Yaquina Bay (mouth of the Yaquina River) on the south, town of Newport on the east and Government Street, Newport, on the north. Today's street address for the Yaquina Bay State Park and Lighthouse is 846 Government Street, Newport, OR 97365.

HISTORIC YAQUINA
BAY LIGHTHOUSE
ACTIVE 1871-1874
TOURS - WEDDINGS
GIFT SHOP
OPEN SAT - SUN
12 - 4 P.M.

There was a period when the old lighthouse was used as quarters for the U. S. Life Saving Service. (Lower) A souvenir button from the Gift Shop.

11

Yaquina Bay Lighthouse and U. S. Coast Guard observation tower 1992.

1. What is a Lighthouse?

light-house / lit-haus / n : a structure
(as a tower) with a powerful light that
gives a continuous or intermittent
signal to navigation.

While *Webster's Collegiate Dictionary* does a good job in just one sentence, there is much more to a lighthouse than that.

From early times, a mariner had to depend on daylight and the ability to see features of the shore in order to recognize where he was. Nightfall brings complete darkness upon the waters and there are no landmarks visible for a vessel's safety.

As bigger and better boats were developed and began to venture further out to sea, lights became the most important factor for night-time safety to mariners.

The first lighted aids to navigation were bonfires built on headlands to guide fishermen home. Later, a combination of pitch

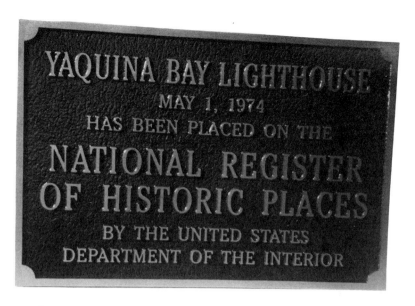

and oakum was burned in an open brazier. In time, olive oil became the fuel.

The Egyptians built the Great Pharos of Alexandria, in Egypt, about 280 BC. This was a 450-foot high lighthouse and was considered one of the Seven Wonders of the Ancient World and guarded the entrance of the Nile River. After standing some 1600 years, it was destroyed by an earthquake in 1302 A.D. From drawings, it appears to have been a tower of white marble with a ramp leading to the top where a beacon fire was kept burning day and night.

Fuels

As we have seen, fuels progressed from pitch and oakum to coal-candles, whale oil, petroleum, coal gas, acetylene. gas, mineral oil, kerosene under pressure and finally electricity.

Where direct connections with electric power lines was not possible, batteries backed by generators powered with gasoline or diesel engines were used.

For a time, the west coast of the United States used what were known as Post Lanterns. This was a lens lantern suspended from an arm projecting from a post (pole) at an elevation of eight to ten feet above the ground. This was effective but the visibility was limited to about one mile even in clear weather.

Locations

Lighthouses are situated at locations where they will be the most helpful for the safe navigation of vessels. These places can be on rocky headlands; reefs; lonely islands; sea-grit rocks; on sand spits; on forts; on top of houses; in prison compounds; in villages; nestled among sand dune grasses; on pilings in bays or sounds or in rivers and along straits.

Examples:
Headlands, Yaquina Head (Ore.)
Reefs, St. George Reef (Crescent City, Calif.)
Lonely islands, Farallon Islands (off San Francisco, Calif.)
Sea-grit rocks, Tillamook Rock (Ore.)
Sand spit, New Dungeness Light (Wash.)
Fort or on top of houses, Point Adams lighthouse (disc.)
    at Fort Stevens (Ore.)
In prisons, Alcatraz Isl. (Calif.)
In villages, Barnegat Light (NJ.)
In sand dune grass, Westport (Wash.)
On pilings, Desdemona Sands (disc.) (Ore.)
Bays, Willapa Bay (Wash.)
Sounds, Alki Point, Puget Sound (Wash.)
Rivers, Warrior Rock Lighthouse Sauvie Island (disc.)
    Columbia River (Ore.)
Straits, New Dungeness Light (Wash.).

2. The Fresnel Lens

By 1871 when Yaquina Bay Lighthouse was built, as well as its neighbor Yaquina Head Lighthouse in 1873, the Fresnel lens had become the standard instrument for supplying the powerful beam of light needed in sea-front lighthouses. The design and placement of the lenses was the invention of Augustin Fresnel (pron: frey-nell).

Fresnel was born in France on May 10, 1788 at Broglie. As a young student, he was not among the scholars for at the age of 8 he still could not read. In his early teen years he suddenly "caught on" when he was led into the field of mathematics. In 1804, at 16½, he entered Ecole Polytechnique. Here he became brilliant in geometry and in the graphic arts. He was fascinated with transmission of rays of light and in 1814, working as an engineer in Paris, prepared a paper on the aberration of light. But that work was not published. He did another paper on diffraction of light which brought him the prize of the Académie des Sciences at Paris in 1818.

In 1819, now 31, he became commissioner of lighthouses and constructed the first compound lenses for use in lighthouses. Confronted with the challenge of developing more powerful lights than the mirror system then commonly used, he invented the system of lenses that was quickly called "The Fresnel Lens." His lens (1821) became world-famous in very short order. This lens refracted and reflected light through hand-ground and polished prisms mounted in cages of brass or bronze. Fresnel's invention was almost instantly acclaimed the best in pharology making earlier devised methods obsolete. Augustin Fresnel died when only 39, of tuberculosis, in 1827.

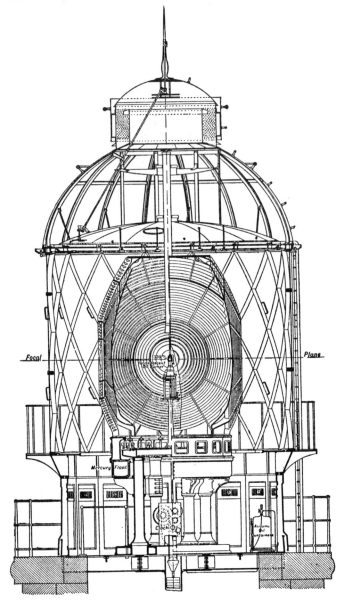

Classic *Fresnel*-design dioptric lens and operating mechanism atop tower. Lantern house surrounds a central bulls-eye lens with a series of concentric glass prismatic rings. By adding triangular prism sections above and below the main lens, it steepened the angle of incidence at which rays shining up and down (lost light) could be collected and made to emerge horizontally. All the collected light emerged through the bulls-eye as a narrow, horizontal pencil-like beam. This is known as the full *Fresnel catadioptric system.*

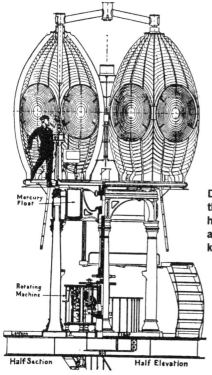

Mercury Float
Rotating Machine
Lantern
Half Section
Half Elevation

Double-lens system produces double the amount of light. Drawing is shown here to illustrate height of 1st Order apparatus compared to height of keeper.

This table lists the principal sizes of the Fresnel lens. The actual size of a lens is expressed by its inside diameter and each is identified by "Order" of size:

Order	Focal Distance (radius)	Diameter (inches)	Range (miles)*	Height (inches)
1st	920mm	72 7/16	22	116 Yaquina Hd†
2nd	700mm	56	20	73
3rd	500mm	39 1/2	18	56
3 1/2	375mm	(not available)	16	(not available)
4th	250mm	20	14	28
5th	187.5mm	14 1/2	12	20
6th	150mm	11 3/16	10	17

There are two supplemental sizes: "Hyper-radial" can be seen 30 miles and Meso-Radial, range 26 miles. Neither are used in the United States. People often asked how "tall" are the various lenses? Here are the heights of the lenses (not the base or pedistal) in Coast Guard Manual *CG222 Aids-to-Navigation*, 1953.

† 1st Order lens, Yaquina Head lighthouse: Base 19½ inches + pedistal 80 inches + lens = approx 18 feet tall.

---

* The range (distance) the light can be seen from a particular order of lens varies due to the type of *lamp* installed; *atmospheric transmistivity* at the area of the lighthouse; *characteristic* and *elevation* of the focal plane of the lens above sea level. *Atmospheric transmistivity* is the cleanliness of the air. Hawaii, as example, is generally excellent while New York City would often be poor. "Cleanliness" should not be confused with the light-scattering effect of fog. In heavy fog, a light, regardless of power, can not be seen very far if at all.

Lighthouses along the Oregon coast were equipped as:

Cape Blanco	1st order
Coquille River	4th order
Cape Arago	4th order
Umpqua River	1st order
Heceta Head	1st order
Cleft of the Rock	Acrylic bulls eye
Yaquina Bay	5th order
Yaquina Head	1st order
Cape Meares	1st order
Tillamook Rock	1st order
Point Adams	4th order
Desdemona Sands	4th order
Cape Disappointment	4th order *

—from Gibbs, *Oregon's Seacoast Lighthouses*

The location and purpose of the lighthouse determined the "order" of the lens that was appropriate. It should be pointed out that how far a light can be seen at sea is dependent on several factors. These include height above sea level, the power of the light emitted as well as cleanliness of the air and weather conditions. The sea-front lighthouses in Oregon are mostly fairly high elevations and are 1st order apparatus. Harbor entrance lights generally need not be seen as far hence are lower order.**

The chore of keeping a light burning during the night was left to light-keepers. These men, and a very few women, in the earliest times had to stay awake all night watching the light to make certain it did not go out. As time passed, various mechanisms were introduced to sound alarms if the light went out. Many of the lights were fixed (non-revolving) position. Others turned on a mechanism that resembled the works of a grand-father clock using weights and gears. Should the mechanism stop during the night, the light-keeper used a crank to keep the light revolving until daylight when repairs could be made. ◊

(Left page) This 5th Order fixed lens is the size and design of the lens that was used in Yaquina Bay Lighthouse. This lens is from the lighthouse on Isle au Haut, Robinson Point, Stonington, Maine. It is exhibited in the Shore Village Museum (Maine's Lighthouse Museum), Rockland, Maine.

* Please turn to page 29 for details.

**The explanations here are "popular" in nature. For technical data, readers are referred to *Encyclopedia Britannica* 11th Edition (1910) Vol. 16. pages 638ff. —Editor

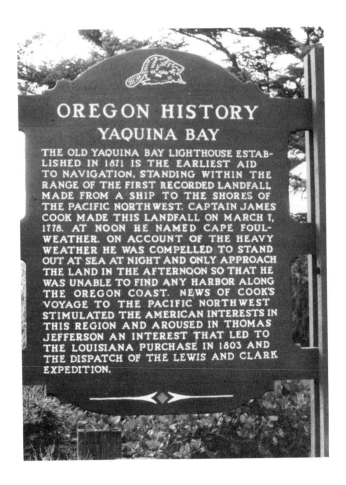

OREGON HISTORY
YAQUINA BAY

THE OLD YAQUINA BAY LIGHTHOUSE ESTAB-
LISHED IN 1871 IS THE EARLIEST AID
TO NAVIGATION, STANDING WITHIN THE
RANGE OF THE FIRST RECORDED LANDFALL
MADE FROM A SHIP TO THE SHORES OF
THE PACIFIC NORTHWEST. CAPTAIN JAMES
COOK MADE THIS LANDFALL ON MARCH 7,
1778. AT NOON HE NAMED CAPE FOUL-
WEATHER. ON ACCOUNT OF THE HEAVY
WEATHER HE WAS COMPELLED TO STAND
OUT AT SEA AT NIGHT AND ONLY APPROACH
THE LAND IN THE AFTERNOON SO THAT HE
WAS UNABLE TO FIND ANY HARBOR ALONG
THE OREGON COAST. NEWS OF COOK'S
VOYAGE TO THE PACIFIC NORTHWEST
STIMULATED THE AMERICAN INTERESTS IN
THIS REGION AND AROUSED IN THOMAS
JEFFERSON AN INTEREST THAT LED TO
THE LOUISIANA PURCHASE IN 1803 AND
THE DISPATCH OF THE LEWIS AND CLARK
EXPEDITION.

Historical Marker at Yaquina Bay State Park.

Footnote to the historical marker.

It is often difficult to "tell the whole story" of an activity of major historical importance in a few lines, well-intentioned as they may be, on a roadside marker. To say "News of Cook's voyage ... aroused in Thomas Jefferson an interest that led to the Louisiana Purchase in 1803 and the dispatch of the Lewis and Clark Expedition" does not "tell the whole story." In short, the U. S. had no plans about the French-held territory that became the Louisiana Purchase. The Americans only sought to acquire New Orleans Island and Florida from France. But France wanted out of its entire holdings on the North American continent and told the U. S. it could buy it all but at what became a tremendous unplanned cost-overrun. The purchase was made without authority and President Jefferson was amazed when his delegates returned to the U.S. and told him what they'd done. The Lewis and Clark Expedition came about because President Jefferson needed to have an on-site report of what he had just bought. Added details, which are intriguing as well as enlightening, can be found in *Flagstaff Hill*. See bibliography. —bw

20

3. What's Been Happening in the Yaquina Bay Area

Two ships, the *Resolution* and the *Discovery*, commanded by Captain James Cook, made their first landfall on the North American continent at the latitude of Yaquina Bay on March 7, 1778. Because of foul weather, he really didn't know where he was. The need for a lighthouse was immediately obvious because ship captains wanted a checkpoint to know where they were. Because of "foul weather" – the captain liked the phrase and used it several times – he did not put down any boats and did not venture ashore. Years later, when claims were being made to the lands of the Pacific Northwest, Captain Cook's failure to step ashore contributed to England's loss. But Cook was not forgotten.

In 1955, the Oregon State Highway Department set up a historical marker to Captain Cook in front of the old lighthouse. The next year the marker was dedicated by the Lincoln County Historical Society.

President George Washington signed a bill that authorized the building of lighthouses along the American coast. Of course at that time, only the Atlantic coast was involved. After Oregon gained statehood in 1859, steps were taken to build lighthouses along its coast due to many shipwrecks. Several come to mind:

1841	*USS Peacock*	1852	*Juliet*
1846	*USS Shark*	1853	*Joseph Warren*
1848	*Maine*	1864	*Cornelia Terry*
1849	*Josephine*	1865	*Doyle*

This lighthouse was specifically a guide for ships at the mouth of the Yaquina River. But with visibility only 11 miles on a good night with its 5th order lens, ships had difficulty with the approach to the river because of the headlands extending to the north. The lighthouse operated only three years until the much brighter – seen 19 miles with 1st order lens – Yaquina Head

Sir Francis Drake, English Maritime Explorer, who wrote that in the area of Oregon he encountered "...vile, thicke and stinking fogges."

light-house, 3½ miles north, lit its light on October 1, 1874.

Also on the Cook voyage, as an observer, was John Ledyard, an American. He later talked with Thomas Jefferson, while they were in Paris, telling him of the area. This aroused Jefferson's interest in the West which, in part, eventually led to the Lewis and Clark expedition (1803-1806). This was the first American exploration from the Mississippi River to the Rocky Mountains. The part of the expedition west from the Rockies to the Pacific Ocean was unofficial.

As early as 1577, the English explorer, Sir Francis Drake, sailed north to somewhere between the 38th and 48th parallels and recorded:

> The rain which fell was an unnatural congealed and frozen substance ... there followed most vile, thicke and stinking fogges.

Apparently the weather was about equal when Captain Cook arrived because he got no closer than about 10 miles off shore. It was at this time he named Cape Foulweather. This was the first geographic feature Cook named on his voyage to the area. While Captain Cook was most direct in his opinion of the weather – "foul" – Lewis L. McArthur, in his *Oregon Geographic Names,* merely identifies the weather as "inclement." Cook also named Cape Perpetua*

---

* McArthur wrote: "It has been frequently asserted that [Cook] named the cape because the bad weather seemed to hold him perpetually in sight of it. But this was not the case [for] he named the headland for St. Perpetua, who was murdered in Carthage on March 7, 203, for it was on St. Perpetua's Day that [Cook] made his discovery.

—*Oregon Geographic Names* 6th Ed. 1992.

While in the area on March 12, he named Cape Gregory, for the saint of that day, but that name was later changed to Cape Arago.

Captain Cook recorded:

The land appeared to be of a moderate height, diversified with hills and vallies, and, almost everywhere, covered with wood. There was, however, no very striking object on any part of it, except one hill, while elevated summit was flat. At the Northern extreme, the land formed a point, which I called Cape Foulweather, from the very bad weather we had, and soon after met with.

Captain Cook was never able to send any boats ashore due to the foul weather so he continued north. Regrettably, for him and for England, he didn't see the Columbia River either – more bad weather? Since he didn't see it, he didn't enter it and he did not mention it. Maybe the weather cleared on the day an American, Captain Robert Gray, ventured by. After trying several times, he forced his ship over the Columbia River bar on May 11, 1792, thus being the first vessel of any nation to enter the long-sought "river of the west."

In 1826, fur trapper Archibald Mcleod and his men camped along the south side of Yaquina Bay. They were looking for beaver. Mcleod did some trading with Indians which they called the "Yacona" tribe.* The trappers stayed about 10 days in the area and discovered many villages on both sides of the bay. These Indians did not have horses therefore they did not travel far from the coast.

No more was recorded about this area until 1849 when Lt. Theodore Talbot, U. S. Army, arrived. He had been directed to undertake an exploring expedition. His diary, *On His Journey Through Lincoln County and Along the Oregon Coast in 1849*, reveals that the Yaquina River's mouth was only 40 to 50 yards wide and so shallow it could easily be forded at low tide. He described the bluff on the north, where the lighthouse was later built, and the low, sandy dunes on the south.

At this time the central coast of Oregon was very remote. To the south, gold had been discovered and a town sprang up that

---

* Additional data about these Indians is in *Indians Along the Oregon Trail.* See bibliography.

was eventually named Gold Beach. At Coos Bay there was a harbor that was kept busy shipping lumber to the gold fields.

To the north, Astoria was very heavy into the fur trade. Across the nearly impenetrable Coast Range of mountains was the fertile Willamette Valley, the destination of most of the Oregon Trail wagon trains.

In 1852 a ship was wrecked near the entrance to Yaquina Bay which was reported in Salem's *Oregon Statesman*:

> Cap't Collins of the schooner *Juliet* who visited Aquinna Bay during his captivity, informs us that he found there ... a fine river, navigable for vessels drawing six or eight feet of water a distance of 20 miles ... but from the appearance he deemed the inlet to be a bad one. He says that the river abounds with oysters, clams and fish of all kinds. The land is level and highly productive. The timber has been nearly all destroyed by fire. None of the land in the vicinity has been claimed yet. *

Digging shellfish at Yaquina Bay. Bridge (Highway 101) over the bay in background.

The first vessel in recorded history to enter Yaquina Bay was the *Calamet* in 1856. It carried supplies for the Siletz garrison which was part of the Grande Ronde Indian Reservation. The reservation covered an area from the Siuslaw River to Tillamook and from the ocean to the summit of the Coast Range. By this

* In the early years there were arguments as to who discovered the succulent Yaquina Bay oysters. In one incident, reported in The *Oregon Statesman* for June 15, 1852, Cyrus Olney, in what some believe to have been an attempt to 'protect" Yaquina Bay oysters from outside gatherers, declared "bf oysters in particular, we saw no signs, not even a fragment of a shell about the lodges or on the beach..." —Editor

Captain Collins, His ship *Juliet*, and Yaquina Oysters

The schooner *Juliet* left San Francisco in mid-January 1852 for the Columbia River but was driven ashore near Yaquina Bay on January 28, so reads an article in the *Oregon Statesman* for March 2.

Although there were efforts to salvage the cargo, the ship was wrecked by the severe winter storms and nothing was saved other than some incidentals.

Having sent an Indian to Oregon City as a messenger soliciting help, Captain Collins, while awaiting the relief party, studied Yaquina Bay. A story in the *Oregon Statesman* on April 6, 1852 provides this information:

Capt. Collins, of the schooner *Juliet,* who visited Aquina Bay during his captivity, informs us that he found there a fine river, navigable for vessels drawing six or eight feet of water a distance of 20 miles. But from the appearance he deemed the inlet to be a bad one. He says that the river abounds with oysters, clams and fish of all kinds. The timber has nearly been nearly all destroyed by fire.

Accordingly, historians have determined that Captain Collins of the *Juliet* was the discoverer of oysters in Yaquina Bay and River.

In the *History of the Native Oysters* we find:

In those kitchens midden deposits adjacent to the natural oyster beds, particularly in places such as Rocky Point, where today a few rocks exposed at low tide, native oyster shells are present along with the more numerous shells of the indigenous mollusks, including the bay mussel (*mytilus edulis*) the cockle (*cardium corbis*); the littleneck clams (*paphia staminea*) and the horse or gaper clam (*Schitzothaeus muttallii*). Apparently Indians collected only a few oysters for food previous to 1812 in those locations in which oysters were exposed at low tide, since most of the natural oyster beds in this estuary are in relatively deep water covered at low tide.

—R. E. Dimick, George Egland and J. B.Long

Did the Indians eat oysters? Although there is argument and some investigations with conflicting statements, it would appear that Indians were eating Yaquina Bay oysters long before the arrival of white men.

time, the Yaquina Indians had been quartered at the Siletz garrison and government agents had been sent to guard the area. As the only easy access was by sea, the *Calamet* made supply voyages.

Several years later, an Indian showed a man by the name of Captain Spencer where the oyster beds were. It was somewhat like leaking news of the discovery of gold for in no time at all, ships began to arrive from San Francisco to haul this delicacy back to the city by the Golden Gate for the *elite* to eat.

During the period of exploitation, there were terrible confrontations between the Indians and the oyster men as to who owned the oyster beds. (The Indians won.) This uproar brought Yaquina Bay to the attention of many outsiders. By 1864, a wagon road had been rammed through the forest and reached from Corvallis to Elk City which was the head of tidewater.

The way to get to the Newport area from Elk City was by water. Great pains were taken for linking the Willamette Valley with the coast by rail. It was in 1885 that the Oregon Pacific Railroad, originating in Corvallis, ran trains to Yaquina City on the eastern edge of today's Newport.

On July 2, 1868, the United States Post Office opened in Newport and was established on the north side of the bay. The first postmaster was Samuel Chase. This was the first post office on Yaquina Bay and was the first in what would become Lincoln County.

In some people's minds, the area was destined to become the "San Francisco of Oregon." This never happened for numerous reasons but a major one was that while San Francisco-bound ships enter the bay there through the one-mile-wide Golden Gate, the only way in to Yaquina Bay is the narrow mouth of the river, over a dangerous bar, that had no distinctive harbor improvements until recent times. The need for a survey of the bay did not get under way until 1868.

Land Rush

In 1866, Yaquina Bay was separated from the Grand Ronde Indian Reservation and the area between Cape Foulweather and Alsea was opened to white settlers. And come they did.

On March 27, 1869, Congress appropriated funds for harbor lights, buoys and two lighthouses. But shipping did not wait for the lighthouse to be built. On May 30, 1870, the steamer *Shubrick* entered the bay and proved that the area could be used for steamer trade. As a result, lumber mills were built and allied businesses sprang up.

The year 1871 saw the opening of the Yaquina Bay Lighthouse on the bluff overlooking the entrance to the bay. It enjoyed a very short life for it was discontinued `in 1874 when Yaquina Head Lighthouse opened, 3 miles north and better positioned for the needs of shipping.

The *Notice To Mariners* published these instructions for

entering Yaquina Bay:

The North shore or "head" of Yaquina entrance consists of a bluff 130 feet high of sandstone formation showing yellow from the sea. The bluff is crowned with an isolated grove of pine or fir trees, some dead and some alive. On its seaward side a beacon or signal has been erected ... directly under it and extending toward the bar is a flat rock oblong in shape.

The south beach is low and sandy, backed by sand dunes, and still further back by a low range of hills bare of timber....

The bar is formed partly by a sand spit making out from the south beach and partly by a double reef of rocks extending from the North head. Between the sand spit and this reef runs the north, or rather the only well-defined channel existing at this present time. Through this channel, choosing the best water, vessels will not get a shoaler cast than 9 feet at mean low water, or 16½ feet to 17 feet at mean high water.... The shoal water in crossing the bar through the channel continues so short a distance and the channel itself is so straight and well defined in ordinary weather, that with a pilot or chart to guide them, vessels draw 10, 12 or 15 feet can, by choosing the time of tide, enter and depart with perfect safety.

Vessels bound for Yaquina Bay, after making the landmarks Seal Rocks, Cape Foulweather, Yaquina Head, South Beach, etc., should not run closer than 12 fathoms until they get the signal on the Light House Point (Yaquina Bay Light) to north-east-a-quarter-east; then run for it until range signals are on.

The range signals are a beacon light erected behind the sand dunes directly back of the beach, and the flagstaff on the hill behind. These are to be kept in range until the water deepens to 3 fathoms and the side of the bay bears north-by-east-a-half-east; then run for it until opposite the town.

In June 1880, the federal government appropriated $40,000 for improvements to Yaquina Bay. Following a new survey, it was determined there were actually three different channels into the bay. These became known as North, Central and South channels but none were considered suitable for safe navigation.

The sand spit to the south had appreciable build up. The channel on the north became studded with rocks. The channel in the center was the shallowest. Since the earlier survey, the ocean had built up the sand and tossed in some rocks to complicate matters. Due to these factors, shipping had come to a near stand-still. In turn, business in the bay communities had also ground to a halt. The harbor entrance was now considered so dangerous that no tug boat captain was willing to risk the his boat or his barges to this harbor entrance.

In an effort to overcome this unruly entrance, a special tug

Yaquina Bay Bridge as viewed from Yaquina Bay State Park.

boat was built in San Francisco and started service on May 29, 1881. The cost of the boat was divided between businesses on Coos Bay and Yaquina Bay. But this tug did not prevent tragedy for in a single day three men drowned trying to locate the best channel trying to get in to Yaquina Bay.

There seemed no way to overcome these challenges short of major harbor improvements. Accordingly, the U. S. Army Corps of Engineers was invited to study the harbor and make recommendations. The intriguing story about this, including the trials and errors, is in the chapter "Harbor Improvements."

As we have seen, there has been a road and a railroad between the Willamette Valley and the coast at Newport for many years. But access between communities along the sea-front was severely hampered because of no through road and the travelers had to drive their horse-drawn wagons on the beaches. In 1913, to prohibit people who owned property abutting the beaches from fencing parts of the beaches, the legislature declared all ocean beaches to be public highways. In recent years, because of congestion on the more popular beaches over right-of-way between walkers and vehicles, the 1965 legislature redesignated the beaches as state-owned "recreation areas." This way motor vehicles could be banned from selected areas. (The official state road map issued every year shows which beaches are closed to motor vehicles.)

28

The old wagon road around Hug Point is now tourist and photographer's attraction.

At one place along the north coast in the early days, at Hug Point, a wagon-wide roadway was chipped out of solid rock to allow passage during high tide around the point. (This remains today and is a great place for photographers.) At low tide, walkers, horsemen and wagons took to the sand.

After much piece-meal construction, final links were made in the coast highway in 1932 except for several major bridges which were completed between 1936 and 1938. The great bridge across the mouth of Yaquina Bay was opened in 1936 amid much fanfare. ◊

Please refer to list of lighthouses and text on page 19.
Cape Disappointment lighthouse opened with a 1st order fixed lens. When North Head Lighthouse, nearby, was opened, the lens from Cape "D" was presumed to have been moved to North Head then a 4th order lens was installed at Cape "D." At this writing, there is a fixed 1st order lens on exhibit in an interpretative center between these two lighthouses. According to Wayne Wheeler, Executive Director of the United States Lighthouse Society, San Francisco, the *Light List* for 1896 shows Cape "D" with a 1st order lens and mentions North Head lighthouse was "to be built." The *Notice to Mariners* for May 16, 1898 shows North Head with a fixed 1st order lens but does not reveal from where it came. The *Light List* for 1900 identifies Cape "D" with a 4th order lens and North Head with a fixed 1st order lens. While firm documentation has not reached the publisher, the circumstances suggest that the lens on exhibit is the original Fresnel from Cape Disappointment. —bw

Jetties at Yaquina Bay (top). Building jetties by hauling rock with trucks and in the earliest days, by steam-railroad.

4. Harbor Improvements

Finally, a 2,500 feet long south jetty constructed of timber cribs filled with brush and straw mattresses surrounded with stone was tried. (The sandstone quarry was 14 miles upriver from Elk River.) This stone proved unsuitable. As this was the first jetty project along the Oregon Coast, every move was a gamble. Mistakes were made and when observed, it was a case of "back to the drawing board." Another quarry site in the Cascade Mountains at the summit of Santiam Pass proved better. This was basalt, a volcanic rock that was significantly resistant to the crashing of winter's angry ocean storms.

The jetty had to be increased to 4,000 feet so the work was not completed until 1889. With the jetty in place, the ocean created two, 13-feet deep channels at the bay entrance but the channels kept shifting. Due to this, the Corps of Engineers approved plans to start on a north jetty. This was begun in December 1888.* The two jetties would be 1,000 feet apart with a 500 foot channel between.

Because the lighthouse on the bluff had been abandoned, it was reconditioned as quarters for the jetty workers.

Over the interveening winters of construction, the stormy sea crashed into the jetty sending some of its rocks flying. (It still does at this writing!) Re-inforcements were needed so more rock was added and the jetties were widened. The outer 750-feet were to be 30-feet wide and 5-feet 4-inches above high water.

Then it was decided to dredge the channel to 30-feet at low

---

* In 1911, the Port of Tillamook, Oregon wrote to the Corps of Engineers that the Port would contribute to the costs of a north jetty at mouth of the bay. The Corps insisted that two jetties was recommended and a single jetty would not work citing other instances along the northwest coast – Yaquina Bay. In Tillamook, the people, with the politicians, forced the Corps to build a single jetty. This jetty proved, in later years, to have been the major cause of the destruction, by coastal erosion, of the Tillamook Spit and the loss of nearly the entire town of Bayocean. The first building on the spit disintegrated 13 years post-jetty (in the 1930s) then the spit was crashed through in a terriffic winter storm with a 1-mile-wide gap, in 1952. The last house fell in 1961. Finally, a second jetty was built and the erosion stopped. For the amazing story read: *Bayocean, The Oregon Town That Fell Into the Sea.* See bibliography.

water. The only way now to accomplish this was to build a spur jetty and extend the main jetties. Finally the project was completed in 1896 – 16 years later – with a cost over-run of $675.000. The total cost was $715,000.

But jetties, always subject to damage by the ocean they penetrate, must have continuing repairs and associated costs. The Corps of Engineers dredge *Yaquina* makes periodic repairs to the system. The Corps added an additional 470-feet to the north jetty in 1988 to improve bar conditions during winter storms.

At the present time, boating is active in the channel mainly by fishing and pleasure boats but there are occasional freighters.

The United States Coast Guard has traditionally maintained a major Search and Rescue base on Yaquina Bay as well as the U. S. Life Saving Service before that. ◊

The U.S. Live Saving Service maintained an early headquarters, boathouse and crew at the beach just south of Yaquina Bay; would work from the lighthouse, with boathouse on north side of bay after lighthouse was discontinued.

5. The Lighthouse Board and Duties of Keepers

In 1889 the U. S. Lighthouse Board declared:

The theory of coast lighting is that each coast shall be so set with towers that the rays from their lights shall meet and pass each other so that a vessel on the coast shall never be out of sight of a light, and there shall be no dark places between lights.

The Lighthouse Service, is considered to be the earliest public work of the United States having been provided for in the first session of Congress in 1789. In 1852 it became known as the Light-House board. This consisted of high-ranking naval officers, army engineer officers and two civilians "of high scientific attainments." The Board was supervised by the Secretary of the Treasury. This Board determined the Lighthouse Districts and appointed Army and Navy officers to be Lighthouse Inspectors. In addition, the Board was responsible for plans and construction of lighthouses, the vessels that would supply the lighthouses and all the buoys and other aids to navigation.

The Board also was responsible for classification and "signature" of the lights. How bright would a light be? How many times and in what colors would it flash – its "signature."

Other of the chores of the inspectors was to maintain discipline of the light keepers and to make certain the prescribed duties were carried out with facility.*

Light keepers had to be between 18 and 50 years old. They had to be able to read, write and keep account books. The health of the keepers had to be good as they were responsible for all physical labor needed at the lighthouse. They needed to be mechanically competent as emergency repairs were their responsibility

---

* In 1883 the Light House Board ordained that all keepers were to be in government uniforms and there would be stiff penalties should an inspector arrive and find the keeper not properly dressed. The rule included such isolated off-shore stations as St. George Reef (Calif.), Destruction Island (Wash.) and Tillamook Rock (Ore.) where just about no one wore a uniform until after the Coast Guard took over the lighthouses.

not only for the apparatus but for the lighthouse itself.

They had to know how to wield a mop as well as a paint brush for the outside as well as the inside of the premises had to be kept clean and looking good.

Some lighthouses built on rocks in the sea had boats and the keepers had to be competent boatmen.

Every effort had to be made to economize throughout the organization which covered all the Atlantic, Gulf and Pacific coasts. When electricity became available – and it was a long time before some lighthouses got it – the oil lamps were discontinued which also eliminated the tedious work of wick trimming, polishing lamp chimneys and the very hazardous storage of the oil.

Those lighthouses with land around them needed to have the land put to good use so keepers were encouraged to grow gardens. It was the keeper and his wife, and possibly children, that tended the gardens. Some light stations were some distance from settlements thus there were barns, horses and cattle.

At some locations, where there was a head keeper and assistant keepers, usually all with wives and families, these folks became a small community. For a while, the postoffice at Barnegat, Oregon operated from the Cape Meares Lighthouse. Yaquina Bay Lighthouse was a one-man-with-wife-and-family operation. There was a garden area and a barn.

The Lighthouse Tender *Shubrick* stopped in Yaquina Bay once a quarter with supplies for the station. On board was the Lighthouse Inspector. He was required to make quarterly visits and he often brought a "traveling library" with him. These were wooden cases of books that could be displayed on a table or, with the lid closed, were instantly ready for transport. The collection numbered about 50 books and included fiction, non-fiction, poetry, scientific works, prayer books and the Bible.

Light keepers were required to keep a log of daily occurrences. Although the National Archives claims to have the Yaquina Bay Lighthouse Log, a worker regrets that it can't be found. ◊

6. The Building of a Lighthouse

Before a lighthouse can be established in a particular place, there has to be a clearly defined need. In the earliest years, the need for installing lights in certain places was well known to ship captains and they often let the government know in no uncertain language where these locations were. In due time the government authorized then built the lighthouses.

Communities on bays or inlets, or at the mouths of rivers, whose people thought they needed a ;lighthouse approached their congressmen. In turn, the House or Senate referred these petitions to the Committee on Commerce which asked the opinion of the Secretary of the Treasury. After this, the Light-House Board ordered an inspector and the engineer of the district concerned to confer then report on the necessity and the expected cost of the proposed light. After these steps, the procedure reversed itself: The report went back to the Secretary of the Treasury then to the Committee on Commerce and on to the House or Senate. If favorable, Congress acts upon the recommendation and *viola!* – a lighthouse is eventually built.

> When the importance of overlapping of light beams was realized, all of the Oregon coast was lighted.

On March 27th, 1869, congress set aside money for harbor lights, buoys and two lighthouses for the Yaquina bay area. One was to be a harbor entrance light. It was not until 1871 however, that they started construction of the first one – the Yaquina Bay Lighthouse – the harbor entrance light.

At the north side of the entrance to Yaquina Bay was a knoll, a perfect location setting for the entrance light. The property belonged to Lester F. and Sophronia S. Baldwin who were early pioneers in the area. They had received title to this hand from the U. S. government in October of 1868. But in 1871, they sold the

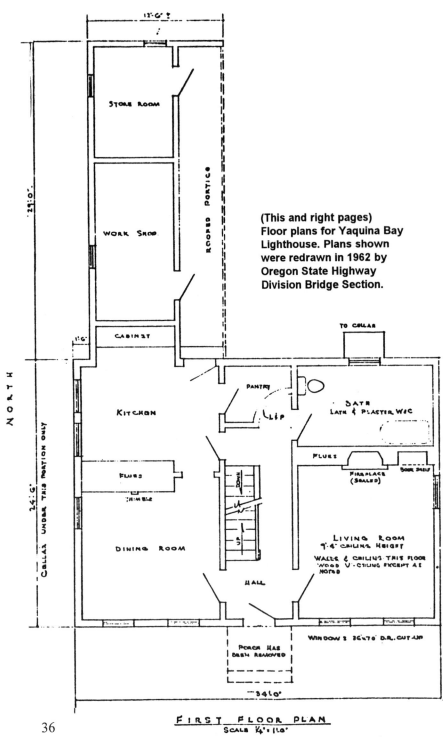

(This and right pages) Floor plans for Yaquina Bay Lighthouse. Plans shown were redrawn in 1962 by Oregon State Highway Division Bridge Section.

FIRST FLOOR PLAN
SCALE 1/4" = 1'0"
SKETCH IS APPROXIMATE, MADE FROM ROUGH MEASUREMENTS

36

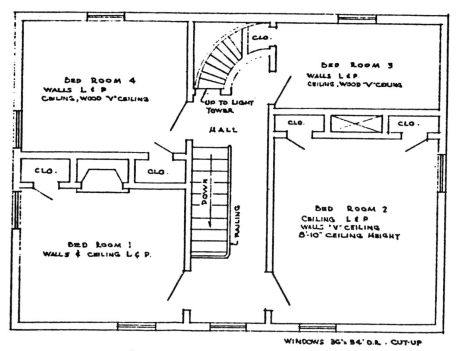

SECOND FLOOR PLAN

36 acres back to the government for $500 in gold coin. The deed is dated January 11, 1871. There is also an attached statement to the deed that:

> Sophorina S Baldwin, wife of L. T. Baldwin, on examination separately and apart from her said husband, acknowledged that she executed this instrument freely without fear or compulsion from anyone.

Her signature was notarized by A. W. Wright, Notary Public.

R. S. Williamson, of San Francisco, a U. S. Lighthouse Engineer, drew the plans for the lighthouse. In fact, two different planes were drawn. The first plan was dated January 30, 1871 and shows a two story structure with four bedrooms upstairs (called "Chambers" in those days) and a parlor, dining room, kitchen, pantry, and oil room on the main floor. The light tower began on the second floor directly above the pantry and rose to a height above the roof line. The plans also included an extension out the back with a storeroom opening off the kitchen. Behind that room there were two more rooms. These were a woodshed and a Water Closet. In our day, the "W.C." is called a bathroom. Both

The original stairs between 1st and 2nd floors of light-house, as seen before re-vitalizing the building during the 1970's.

of these rooms opened directly to the outside. A beautiful stair-case rose from just inside the front door. Another winding staircase led from the second floor to the light tower landing where a tiny watch room was tucked in under the roof.

The other plan was dated March 27, 1871. It called for 1½ stories. The upper floor had only two chambers. These were more like dormitory rooms. The lower floor was arranged backwards from the first plan. There was a smaller extension on the back with no provision for a Water Closet. The tower was arranged nearly the same as was the watch room. Both plans show a basement with stairs going down from the inside.

The first plan was chosen which turned out to be much more suitable for family life.

When a lighthouse was built, very often another one was built using the same plan. The floor plans for the house as well as the parapet and deck plates were for both Yaquina Bay and Trinidad Head Light (California) as noted.

Trinidad light was also built in 1871, but the headland chosen for the placement of this light was so high, all that was needed was a 25 foot tower. The keepers house was separate from

View from rear of lighthouse with shutters closed.

the tower, so I think it is safe to say the plans that were drawn were never used.

There was a flurry of discussion early in 1871 as to how these deck plates and the parapet were to be constructed. We find the following words written on the plans:

"Lantern to be constructed in the East -- the deck plates in California. The size and shape of the five exterior deck plates will depend on the size and shape of the Tower and will be drawn by Col. Williams."

Even though directions had been written on the plans, there was more discussion as we see in the following letters:

> Gen. Duane,
>
> Sir,
>
> I send you a drawing of the bottom of the parapet and deck, as I should make it were I to do it according to my judgment.
>
> In the drawing I have represented the deck in nine pieces, you will see by their (L.H. Board) drawing it is in four pieces.
>
> My object in making it in so many pieces is the convenience of handling them at the tower.
>
> On my drawing, I have shown a full sized section of a portion of the parapet and deck where they will have to make the alteration.
>
> Yours respectfully
> Ira Winn

On the back of Mr. Winns letter Gen. Duane writes to Engineer Secretery.

> L.H.B. Major Elliot:
>
> The enclosed letter and sketch will give all the information any maker will require to make the deck plates for the lantern that I am having made for Cal.
>
> The lantern parapet will be made circular. The pattern had been commenced before I received your letter. I think I can get the lantern shipt by the middle of May. Perhaps before. I would have had a tracing of the enclosed made but have no one to do it for me and I have no time to do it myself.
>
> Yours
>
> J.C.D.

Then Major Elliot writes

> Mr. McMakin:
>
> Gen. Duane is making <u>two</u> lanterns for California. The decks will be made in California and both should be made so that the boxes shipped from the east will not have to be unpacked till they get to their lighthouses which are distant from San Francisco & away from docks of all kinds− hundreds of miles.
>
> It seems to me that the drawings of the plates are not sufficiently in detail & that we shall have trouble as in the Point Reyes* case. Let me know about details as I wanted & I will send it back to Gen. Duane.
>
> (signed)   E.   Mar. 2 1871

The deck was made in four pieces.

Construction was begun on May 1871. Timbers for the lighthouse were hauled from the Wren area by a man named Henry Palmer Harris.

Harris had settled on a homestead at Harris Station, a community along the Marys River near Wren west of Corvallis. He owned a team of horses and it was with these horses and a wagon, that timbers for the sills were hauled from Wren to Newport. At that time, the trail ran past Fort Hoskins, over the coast range to Siletz and down to Toledo. The timbers were then

---

* Point Reyes is about 35 miles northwest of the Golden Gate.

40

loaded on a boat or barge and brought to Newport.

The bricks are believed to have come from the San Francisco Bay area having been ballast on sailing vessels. There does not seem to be written information to confirm this but availability from the ships' holds was the practice in that day when nothing was wasted. The bricks were probably sun-dried on the ground as there are many indentations on them that suggest the shape of grasses and sticks.

Two contracts were let for the building of the lighthouse. One went to Joseph Bein, a Lampist from San Francisco to fit the iron work and lantern together, and contractor. The other went to Ben Simpson of Oneatta, on the Columbia River, as the building contractor.

The lens was ordered around April 4, 1871 and the contract with Mr. Bien was dated June 16, 1871. He was to be paid $100 in gold or its equivalent. The lens was shipped on the lighthouse tender *Shubrick.*

Mr. Simpson was to "furnish all labor and work necessary for completion " and to specify kinds of work and hourly rates of pay. He provided this report:

Masons	.621/2 per hour
Carpenters	.50 per hour
Painters	.50 per hour
Laborers	.25 per hour
Teamsters	
with two-horse wagons .75 per day	

Local help was used in the building of the lighthouse. Except, of course for Mr. Harris.

On November 3, 1871, a light shone from the newly completed harbor entrance lighthouse. It had been fitted with a Fifth Order, non-rotating Fresnel lens. The lens was 2 feet high and 1½ feet wide. The shore side was probably blanked out. (We say probably because we know of no written information regarding this.) It had a single wick lantern and that burned whale oil which showed a white light. The light was approximately 128 feet above sea level. At last the treacherous entrance to Yaquina Bay was being guarded by a light!

This was the first of four wooden-framed combination

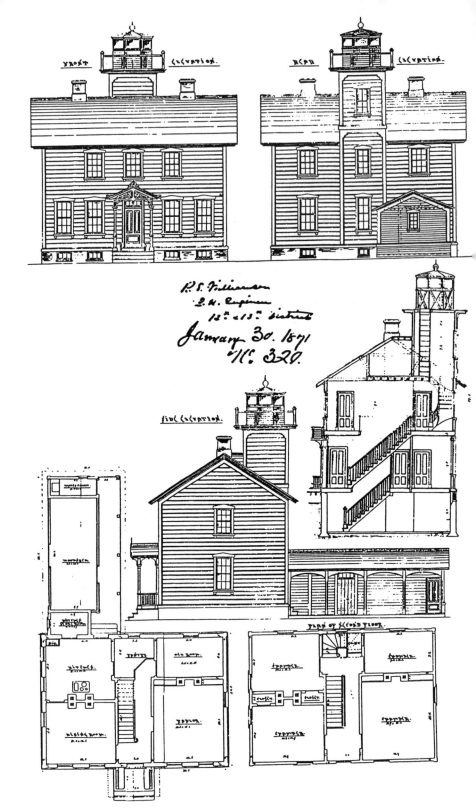

keepers quarters and light tower to be constructed in Oregon and is now the only one left. The others, Point Adams, Desdemona Sands and Willamette River Lights are long gone.

In age, it is second only to the light at Cape Blanco which is one year older. Even though the lighthouses at Umpqua River and Cape Arago were built in 1857 and 1866, those original structures have been destroyed and newer ones have taken their places. Umpqua Light No. 2 was built in 1894 and Cape Arago No. 2 in 1908-09. But as the cape Arago light was at great risk due to erosion. it was replaced by No. 3 in 1934 then No. 2 was later dismantled. *

Yaquina Bay Lighthouse is considered to be the oldest structure in Newport and is on the *National Register of Historic Places*. As such, it is afforded protection in that it cannot be changed or dismantled. ◊

---

* Details of all Oregon sea-front lighthouses are in Jim Gibbs' book *Oregon's Seacoast Ligthouses*. See bibliography.

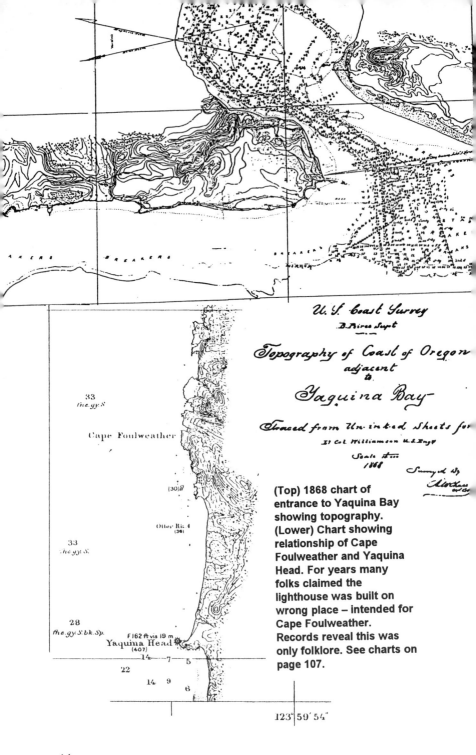

U. S. Coast Survey
B. Pierce Supt

Topography of Coast of Oregon
adjacent
to
Yaquina Bay

Traced from Un-inked Sheets for
It Col. Williamson U.S. Engr

Scale
1868

Surveyed by

33
fine. gy. S

Cape Foulweather

(30)S

Otter Rk. 4
(36)

33
fine. gy. S.

28
fine. gy. S. bk. Sp.

F 162 ft vis 19 m
Yaquina Head
(407)

14   7   5

22

14   9

6

123° 59' 54"

(Top) 1868 chart of entrance to Yaquina Bay showing topography. (Lower) Chart showing relationship of Cape Foulweather and Yaquina Head. For years many folks claimed the lighthouse was built on wrong place – intended for Cape Foulweather. Records reveal this was only folklore. See charts on page 107.

44

Captain Charles H. and Sarah Peirce. His picture was probably made about time he entered Light-house service. Hers, at about age 18-19 in New York.

7. The Keeper at the Lighthouse

Captain Peirce and his wife arrived at the lighthouse with 6 children. When they left, 3 years later, they counted 7. Their youngest, Kate, was born in the lighthouse.

Charles H. Peirce was born in Three Rivers, Massachusetts. He married Sarah A. O'Leary Low July 22, 1850 at No. 6 Perry Street, New York City.

Their children and birth dates:

Charles: Jr. September 11, 1851
Franklin: October 5, 1853
Storie: January 2, 1856
Gertrude: March 6, 1858
Harriet: October 1, 1860

Storer: December 21, 1866
Eugene: April 9, 1868
Sarah: December 3, 1869
Katherine: March 25, 1872

Charles Jr. did not made it to the west coast with the family. At this point, no one knows why. Storie died in infancy.

Mrs. Peirce, Franklin, Gertrude and Harriet traveled by ship around the Horn to meet the Captain on the west coast.

Agnes Daniels, of the Fogarty Creek area, tells us that she remembers her grandmother (Harriet) telling about the trip. Captain Peirce was stationed at the Fort on Alcatraz Island in San Francisco Bay, as well as at Fort Humboldt, near Eureka, also in California, in 1866. It is assumed the ship came to port in San Francisco.

His career as an Army officer finally ended at Fort Tongass in Alaska, where he was in arrest from November 3, 1869 to March 5, 1870. He was to be Court Martialed because of accusations he made accusing an officer of his command of embezzling public funds and for being intoxicated while on duty.

His next stop was Cape Disappointment (Fort Canby), Washington, where he left his family while he traveled to Washington, D. C. where the Court Marshall would be conducted. Then he would be mustered out of the Army.

His life's work had been a career in the Army and now it was over. He appeared to be a gentleman and recognized his obligation to support his family. He started at the top by writing a letter to an old Army acquaintance, who was now President Ulysses S. Grant. At this point, assistance in some civil work assignments was often subject to political appointment.

He did not ask for any specific assignment, just a job doing anything anywhere. It would be interesting to know how he felt about a lighthouse keeper's position should he have been asked. And when he received an appointment as a lighthouse keeper, it must have been quite a jolt. But for his wife and the family, as they had been living in Army camps for the past five years, it must have sounded pretty good. A photograph of Fort Tongass at the time the Peirce family lived there appeared like a primitive hunting camp. After living and working on isolated Army camps, more than one visitor to the lighthouse has remarked that it must have felt to the family as if they were moving into a castle.

He and his family arrived at his new assignment by May 1, 1871. The story has been handed down through the generations of the family that Franklin, the oldest of the Peirce children to live at the lighthouse, also helped in the construction of it.

Almost nothing is known about their stay at the lighthouse. We can only assume they planted a garden in the spot provided on the lower lever. A barn had been provided. so perhaps they bought a cow to provide milk for the children and butter for the table. Their descendants tell us that Mrs. Peirce was a very proper lady who always used a table cloth and napkins. Each member of the family had his own napkin ring. The children were not allowed to talk while they were at the table and were expected

The lighthouse showing picket fence and part of boardwalk that led, over sand, down the back hill toward Newport.

This was a letter written to his father by Charles Jr. when he was nine years old.

West Point, NY

My Dear Papa

I received your affectionate letter on the 12th.

Frank said that he would write if Ma would write letters if Mama would get him a copy and he would send it in Mamas letter. Mr Bittman sent his best respects to you. My teeth are coming in again. Gerty she sent a kiss to you. The river is open so that two boats went up to New Burgh to day. We all send a kiss to you and Mr. Peirce and Mrs. Ayers. Write soon and tell me all a bout the place for we all wish to hear about the place.

Remember your affection ate son Charles H Peirce.

Feb 15th 1861

to eat what was served to them without complaining. It is hard to imagine the amount of work it must have taken for her to keep the house spotless. Remember that a lighthouse inspector could show up, unannounced, at any time and give it the "white-glove" treatment. This "treatment" meant that the inspector, wearing clean white cloves, would run his gloved hand over surfaces in the lighthouse snooping for dust. If he found any, he could, if he wished, hand out demerits. Wives of keepers knew all about this and made a point of maintaining a clean and dustless facility every day of the year.

The Lighthouse Tender *Shubrick* plied the Pacific Coast stopping at each lighthouse. The ship's visit was like a two-pronged pitchfork:

> 1) The visit was always looked forward to because the visit brought supplies to the keepers. As this was a government reservation, the government provided such staples as flour, salt, sugar, beans, etc.
>
> 2) The trip generally brought the Lighthouse Inspector.

Keepers were hard to come by on the west coast because of the isolation at most lighthouses. The surroundings were often pretty severe and there are records of keepers asking to be relieved.* To make the job more attractive, keepers were paid $1,000 per year compared to $400 to $600 for the same duty on the east coast. The western wage seemed a fortune in those days!

For an outgoing man, the lure of gold in the fields made lighthouse tending an unattractive job. On the other hand if the keepers had persistence, "kept their noses clean," and if their wives maintained the place – "spit-and-polished" – the job was secure.

This family has the distinction of being the only keepers of the light at Yaquina, since it shone for only three years. The government elected to decommission the little light at Yaquina Bay soon after the first order light at Yaquina Head was completed thus it became moving time again for the family.

Since there was an opening for a keeper at Cape Blanco on the South Oregon coast, the family was transferred there. Captain Peirce served there until 1883. He was in the Army 24 years plus the Civil Service for 12 years.

In an affidavit recorded in Coos County Oregon, Captain Peirce stated:

> During service as principal keeper at Cape Blanco, I contracted the asthma in 1877 and have been suffering from that disease since that time and am no longer able to perform only very light manual labor about my home, and that my malady does not arise or continue from vicious habits.

He retired to a farm on the Sixes River where he died in 1897.

We found his obituary in a scrapbook at the Oregon Historical Society in Portland, Oregon:

---

* Some examples of this are in *Terrible Tilly; Tillamook Rock Lighthouse*. See bibliography.

48

Charles H. Peirce

Captain C. H. Peirce died at his home on Sixes River, in Curry County, on the 18th of May, at the age of 74.

He served both in the Mexican and Civil War, his public career covering a period of 40 years. After leaving the military service, Captain Peirce entered the lighthouse service, first at Yaquina Bay, and afterward at Cape Blanco, where he served faithfully several years, when declining health admonished him to retire to private life, and he moved with his family to a pleasant and comfortable home on Sixes River.

His widow Sarah continued to live in the area and received money from his pension. Her name was dropped from the pension rolls August 24, 1901. We have not been able to determine her date of death nor where Charles and Sarah are buried.

A Peirce family reunion was held at the lighthouse in early October 1991. Four generations attended ranging in age from 84 to 4 months.

Many of the fifty-some relatives that gathered had never met and until a few years ago and didn't know the others existed

Out of the seven children who grew to adult-hood, only five had children and out of that five, only four branches of the family could be found – those of Franklin, Gertrude, Harriet and Sarah. Kate, the one who was born in the lighthouse, is thought to have moved to the east coast.

It has been interesting to see how the family got together after being scattered for so long. Bob McClain of Albany, Oregon, a great-grandson, visited the lighthouse in the 1970s and signed the guest book. He scribbled a note to anyone who might be related to contact him. Along came Agnes Daniels a great-granddaughter and her daughter, Colleen McLean of Seattle, who saw the note and immediately contacted Bob.

In 1989, two great-grandsons, one from Anchorage, Alaska, the other from Silverdale, Washington, visited the lighthouse and were told about the others. The rest is history. ◊

Members of Life Saving Service were transferred into Coast Guard. Man stands watch duty on top of lighthouse. Note early radio antenna.

Coast Guard Station - Newport Oregon

50

8. People of the Lighthouse

The first people to occupy the lighthouse were Charles and Sarah Peirce (pron: purse) and their children. They moved in to the brand new building in 1871 with their 6 children. When they left, they had 7 as their youngest daughter, Kate, was born there. They moved out in 1874 when the lighthouse was discontinued and Captain Peirce, the keeper, was transferred to Cape Blanco.

In 1888, the Corps of Engineers obtained permission to occupy the lighthouse as living quarters during the construction of the jetties. It was a drawn-out project so they stayed until 1896.

A Mrs. Jane Hume, a widow and her family of 5 children from Minnesota lived in the lighthouse for awhile. Another child, whose father was the superintendent of the railroad roundhouse a distance up the bay, boarded with the family in order to establish local residence in order to attend the Newport school. When these people moved out has not been established.

In 1900, the U. S. Lifesaving Service occupied the lighthouse as crew headquarters and a lookout station.

Ethel Kidd of Toledo, when a small child, and her parents had lived at the lighthouse while the lifesaving crew was there. Her father was in the Lifesaving Service and all married personnel lived in small houses near where the present Coast Guard station is located. (Single men lived in the lighthouse.) She recalled waking up "Lover's Lane" (a pathway up the back side of the hill) with her mother to meet her father when he went off duty. "The boat shed and ways were on the bay-front near where the bridge is now. When there was a rescue to be made, the men had to run down the hill and let the boats down into the bay then head for sea using oars" she recalled.

With the front steps of the lighthouse as her viewing position, she watched Halley's Comet in 1910. Then, while on the inclined boardwalk that went from town up to the lighthouse, she watched

U. S. Life Saving Service station on South Beach.

Boat drill were almost daily occurrences. Men push wheeled cart into surf then lower surfboat into water. (Lower) Wearing cork life jackets, crewmen work the boast into the surf.

53

Crossing line of breakers, the men head out to sea. This was a dangerous but necessary business.

(Top) Modern self-righting 36-foot motor lifeboat was mainstay of modern U. S. Coast Guard for several decades, was replaced by larger 44-foot boat (lower).

the fire that destroyed buildings along the waterfront.

In 1908, Richard Christianson, 17, joined the Lifesaving Service. He tells of having been stationed in the lighthouse. He recalled there were different drills every day. Monday was boat drill; Tuesday, flag drill; Wednesday, resuscitation drill; Thursday, fire drill; Friday breeches buoy drill. These exercises were held every morning unless there was a turnout for rescue duty. Afternoons were occupied at the boat house on the bay with maintenance of equipment.

At the lighthouse, they used the dining room for the Day Room (recreation, library and drills). The furniture was a round table and captain's chairs. There was a small stove in the dining room for heat. The parlor and upstairs bedrooms were furnished with cots (1-man iron bunks) for 8 men. These rooms were heated with fire places. For baths, water was heated in a wash boiler on the stove then two men carried this probably to the store room.

Although the lighthouse had a kitchen, it was never used for cooking. It was used for storage. The pantry off the kitchen was a carpenter shop and for general repairs.

There was someone on duty in the tower 24 hours a day. Life in the U. S. Lifesaving Service was, like being a mud-soldier in the Army – Spartan. Each man had almost a day off every 8th day. They got off from noon until 8 o'clock the next morning. Sunday's were ordinary work days because a ship, caught in the surf or on the rocks, did not choose a particular day on which to be wrecked. The men received a salary and room and board. There was no pension plan.

In 1915, the Lifesaving Service became a part of the United States Coast Guard and continued using the lighthouse until their compound was built on the waterfront in 1927. R. C. Vanhine was a family man with 2 children and was a member of the Coast Guard. He related:

> The skipper and 'No. 1' man, along with 7 enlisted men, were stationed at the lighthouse. They were divided into 4-hour watches and had to punch a time-clock every half-hour. The clock was located at the end of a catwalk that extended 15-feet from the northwest corner of the lighthouse. This was called the 'Key Post.'

The boathouse and launching ways were down the bluff

where the bridge now stands. The boats could be unwieldy in a rough surf but launching at Yaquina Bay, if the rescue call was just off the mouth was easier than launching from a beach directly into the line of breakers. But the lifesavers were trained to do this.

Yaquina Bay Station had one power boat but its size and type of the motor has not been established. The skippers' lived in a building near the boathouse.

Josephine Rogers Patrick, now of Portland whose father was in the Coast Guard, was born in 1908 and arrived in Newport when she was 11. She remembered, with a snicker, that the path up the bluff to the back door to the lighthouse was known as "lover's lane." She also recalled there were only two ways, in those days, to get to Newport. The least expensive and common route from Portland was by boat down the Columbia River, into the ocean then south along the coast to Yaquina Bay. The other was to take a train to Corvallis, change trains then cross the Coast Range Mountains to Yaquina City. From the depot, there was a short walk to the dock then take the small boat for the last 3-miles. Either way was an adventure.

During 1939, Genevieve Stark Lewis also lived in the light-house. Her husband was working for the Highway Department and they were renting a little cabin in Nye Beach. They were invited to move into the lighthouse while the family, who was usually there, made a trip to the Golden Gate International Exposition, the great world's fair in San Francisco.

She remembered always going to the upstairs middle window around 3 o'clock to watch the return of the fishing fleet. The boats seemed to pause a bit then ride the breakers in across the bar.

This couple had little money even for groceries so they gathered their dinners from the sea. She wrote:

There was a road below the lighthouse and from there it was about a 2-foot drop to the dune below that stretched right down to the beach. We were able to dig enough clams for our dinner meal in just a short time. We also went over to the beach on the bay where the Hatfield Marine Science Center is now and dragged a rake behind us. Just under the surface of the sand were all the butter clams we wanted.

Once in awhile Sam Boardman* of Salem, would come over on an

* Samuel Boardman became known as the "Father of Oregon State Parks." Boardman State Park, on the south Oregon Coast, is named for him. For a description of this and all of the Oregon State parks facing the sea-front, refer to *Oregon's Salty Coast*. See bibliography.

inspection tour and would stop by the lighthouse. We first met him at our cabin at Nye Beach. One day we were just having breakfast when he stopped by so we invited him in to join us. Even though I was not a very good cook, he kept coming back and would always bring some ham or bacon or perhaps jam or maple syrup with him. He continued these breakfast visits with us when we were in the lighthouse.

Later, park caretaker Merle Wells and his family lived at the light-house. By that time, the house had been fixed up so it was more comfortable to live in. There was electricity and an indoor bathroom. The fireplaces had been bricked up and Mr. Wells boarded up the stairway to the watch room to conserve heat.

One of his children, Ray, tells that he remembers storms so severe the wind would blow him and his siblings from the back of the house to the gravel parking area.

The two Wells boys shared the upstairs northwest bedroom. Ray recalled the building shaking so badly from the tremendous winds, the bed moved nearly 6-inches away from the wall during one night's storm.

The jetties were not as long then as they are today and the bar was impossible to cross in a bad storm. The weather was so bad that at times the Coast Guard could not respond to a distress call with their boats. The *Ruth Ellen*, a 50-foot fishing vessel, which could get over the stormy bar, was often used for making winter season rescues.

Pearl Harbor Day, December 7, 1941, the "day that shall live in infamy," found the federal government suddenly very interested in reclaiming the lighthouse. It was wanted as an official coastal lookout position. As the U. S. Army Signal Corps had broken the Japanese diplomatic code and was intercepting Japanese secret messages, the American government had reason to suspect that there might be landings of Japanese forces along the northwest coast. The Coast Guard immediately established lookout stations at existing lighthouses and other specific locations on the sea-front, then by September 1942, started a walking Beach Patrol.*

Ray Wells said he seemed to remember the hillside at the lighthouse "bristled with gun emplacements" and the Wells family

---

* See *Silent Siege-III* and *Lakeport* in bibliography.

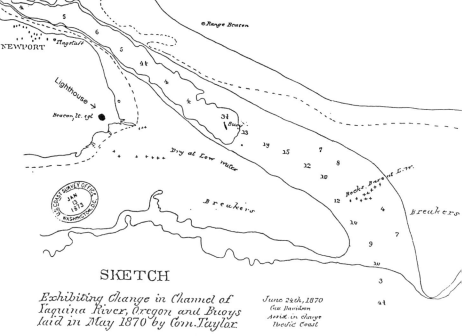

SKETCH

Exhibiting Change in Channel of
Yaquina River, Oregon and Buoys
laid in May 1870 by Com.Taylor

June 24th, 1870
Geo. Davidson
Assist. in charge
Pacific Coast

were the only civilians allowed on the bluff. This was a young boy whose eyes and mind were filled with the wonderment of his home, the lighthouse, suddenly being surrounded by uniformed men carrying guns. We will see more about this in the Chapter "Guns at the Lighthouse,"

In the 1950s and 1960s several other caretakers lived in the lighthouse, none of them, according to newspaper reports, enjoyed their stays very much. Finally, the old relic lighthouse was condemned. Because of public interest – more curiosity than anything else – the Lincoln County Historical Society received permission to fix it up a bit. Between 1965 and 1972 they operated it as a museum and gift shop.

The year 1973 saw the Oregon State Parks Department begin a major restoration of the property including the building. When the work was finished, it was manned by State Parks personnel and reopened again to the public. See the chapter "The Re-Birth of Yaquina Bay Lighthouse."

On July 13, 1988, the Friends of Yaquina Bay Lighthouse was organized by a group of public-spirited citizens to preserve and interpret the lighthouse for the public's interest. Details about this group and its activities is in the chapter "Friends of Yaquina Bay Lighthouse." ◊

In early 1930's, the dilapidated lighthouse was at risk of being demolished. It was not until 1973 than an aggressive restoration project was undertaken.

9. Rebirth of Yaquina Bay Lighthouse

It would be safe to say that no other lighthouse on the Oregon Coast has had such a varied history than this one. It is the shortest-lived lighthouse in Oregon since it was used as a lighthouse only 3 years.

Then it became the headquarters for the jetty construction crew. When they moved out, one family after another lived there more-or-less in a care-taker status. The federal government tried to sell the property but there were no takers. Probably the longest occupancy (to date) was the U. S. Lifesaving Service/U. S. Coast Guard for 32 years. Following this tenure, the light-house was occupied by State Highway and State Parks families along with a few caretakers.

Down through the years minimal repairs were made. At one time, it was thought that with the coming of the railroad in 1885, trade would pick up and ships would once again come into the bay making this a great commercial port. In this event the light-house would surely be lit again. But not so.

This is a good place to discuss the much asked question: "What happened to the lens ?" The answer: We really don't know.

Our friend Jim Gibbs,* a former Coast Guardsman, editor and writer, tells that in his research he found it was the habit of the Lighthouse Board to remove a lens when a lighthouse was de-commissioned. The lens would be warehoused for potential use in another lighthouse.

But we do have a piece of the lighting apparatus. One day in 1989, an unknown person phoned the State Park office and asked if we wanted the old chimney to the lamp that was in the lighthouse. His story is that it was stolen about 1910 by a teen-ager who was to become a prominent citizen of Lincoln City. That person gave it to a resident in 1972, who in turn, presented it

---

* James A. Gibbs has written a number of books dealing with lighthouses along the Pacific Coast. A recent work is the book *Oregon's Seacoast Lighthouses*. See bibliography.

Landscaping was part of the project.
Did the planting take hold? See page 76.

The Coast Guard lookout tower has been part of the scene for decades however no one seems to know just when it was built.

to us. No names were asked. We were pleased to accepted it.

However, there is a great difference between the lens and the lantern. We have a piece of the lantern but we do not have the lens for as we have seen, it was policy in the early days when a lighthouse was discontinued, the lens would be removed for use elsewhere.

After the State of Oregon acquired the property in 1934, many improvements were made in the park. Members of the Civilian Conservation Corps (CCC) set up a camp in the park and worked here from October 1934 to April 1935 then again between October 1935 and April 1936. All of the work plans were approved, supervised and inspected by the National Park Service office in San Francisco.

The CCC crew did these projects:

Built 1 double restroom of rock
Built 1,946 lineal feet of rock guard rail
Installed 4 garbage pits
Installed 5 drinking fountains
Laid 920 feet of water pipe for connection with the Newport city water

Rear view. Shutters were added when the building was restored.

    system
Built 5 fireplaces
Erected 1 one rock monument with a sign
Placed 14 other signs
Built 28 table and bench combinations
Built .6 of a mile of road
Built ¾ of a mile of foot paths
Improved .4 of a mile of the park road
Landscaped 30 acres including moving of or planting 2,463 shrubs and
    trees
Prepared 2,000 square yards of parking area for surfacing
Cleared 5 acres
Seeded and sodded 7 acres of the park.

The lookout tower rises
60 feet and affords an
excellent view of the
seascape to those who
are allowed to be up
there. The public is not.

The State Highway Maintenance crews paved the parking lot.

Right after Pearl Harbor Day (December 7, 1941), the Park was closed for most of World War II but when the threat of Japanese invasion was lessened later in the war, the park was reopened to visitors on May 1, 1944. This opening was of particular importance to local folks who could walk to the park. During the war there was very tight gasoline rationing and, unless one operated a business and required new tires, it was nearly impossible to get a "priority" from a War Production Board for tires.

Even though the lighthouse had been lived in on and off through the years, it had fallen into severe disrepair therefore the Highway Department reached a decision, in 1946, to demolish the building. In making the decision, the bureaucrats had not considered the feelings of the local residents. The locals voiced severe opposition. "Not our lighthouse," they screeched! The Highway Department backed off. Two years later, the Lincoln County Historical Society was organized and the main item on their agenda was to preserve the lighthouse.

In 1955, the Society handed out flyers at the Lincoln County Fair asking the public to vote for funds for the rehabilitation of the lighthouse. Again, in 1955, they were urging the locals to become members of the Society so they would have funding. Again, this was earmarked for the lighthouse.

Some repairs were made but it wasn't until 1965 that their group moved in, operated a museum and gift shop under a 5-year lease with the State Parks Department.

While the society was using the building, they cleaned and patched the interior as best they could but did not have the funds to do extensive refinishing. The lighthouse was inspected by the Richard I. McCosh, Assistant State Parks Superintendent. His report showed the Society to have only limited funds that would prevent carrying out a "comprehensive program at the lighthouse" They (the society) were thinking of having display cases "filled with things to look at," he wrote in his report. His idea however was to showcase the lighthouse as an interpretive exhibit. In other words, show it as it was during its active service as a lighthouse. But there was no lens.

In 1970, the lease was renewed for two years. By the end of that time, State Parks had decided to engage in an extensive restoration project. Ken Lucas, then park manager at Yaquina Bay State Park and Roger Holstein, manager at Beverly Beach State Park would direct this project.

A detailed inspection was made of the lighthouse property on November 28, 1973 for establishing guidelines for the restoration project. The visiting team was:

> Gerald R. Leavitt, Field Operations Supervisor;
> C. H. Lenz, District I Parks Supervisor
> Ken Lucas, Manager Yaquina Bay State Park
> Roger Holstein, Manager of Beverly Beach State Park
> Don Heyen, Architect, Bridge Section
> Elisabeth Walton, Park Historian
> Lyle Warren, Contractor.

The work was to be commenced early in 1974 and finished by April of 1975 to be ready for the summer season. Labor would be done by park personnel but they would not be working on the lighthouse during the 1974 peak summertime season. The total cost of the project was estimated to be between $75,000 and $80,000.

Building codes would be checked, floor plans would be closely studied and precise measurements would be taken. Permits, if needed, would be obtained. Underground electrical service would be installed. There would be tools needed above those in the parks inventory of hand tools.

A list of projects had been made and high on that list was security fencing. The fence was to be concealed as much as possible by natural growth. Three openings were provided: front and rear pedestrian gates and a gate in the back for cars and emergency vehicles.

Provision was made for a furnace so the house could be kept warm as well as dry. Care was taken so the building could be restored to its original condition as much as possible. At some time during the life of the building, the back "ell" extension had been remodeled. Now, with original building plans at hand, it was to be returned to its original size. Where the "Water Closet" had been would be rebuilt as a men's restroom. Part of the old woodshed would be converted into the women's restroom. The remainder would become a storeroom.

The sills and floor joists would be repaired, keeping as much of the original wood as possible. The brick foundation would be repaired as well as the eaves, chimney stacks, and the flues. The windows in the lantern room were re-glazed. The shingle siding that had been put on the south and west sides would be torn off and the original shiplap siding would be replaced as close as possible. It is said that when they removed the bottom siding board, the rest fell off. They had been held in place only by that one bottom board! The originals were determined to be redwood.

The eave troughs also were made of redwood and were in one piece. It took three pieces of cedar, laminated and glued to match the configuration of the old redwood troughs.

After the lighthouse was discontinued, later occupants closed the fireplaces to stop the tremendous down-drafts of wind particularly during winter storms.

Some of the fireplaces were opened, the plumbing was revamped, the electrical wiring was replaced and the outlets were hidden so the house – which was constructed before buildings had electric power – would look as much like the original as possible.

The most worn stair treads were replaced. The banisters were restored and the spindles were either replaced or repaired. It took two Park Department aides two months to remove all the layers of paint from the banisters and spindles. When they finally got down to the bare wood, someone said, "Now let's paint them"! But clear varnish was applied and the banisters are now a showpiece in the lighthouse.

All the old paint was removed from woodwork throughout the lighthouse. It took five 55 gallon barrels of paint remover for this project.

Laths on walls were replaced and a contract was let for re-plastering, where needed. Windows were repaired and replaced. Thresholds were replaced and doors re-hung. The old iron ladder to the tower was found in the basement and it was re-installed.

The grounds outside were cleaned. An old Army command seemed effective: "If it isn't growing pick it up" – and rusty old anchor chains and falling apart whale bones were carried off. When all was finished, a coat of sparkling white paint was applied. Yaquina Bay Lighthouse had come back to life!

Then began the discussions regarding the furnishings. Current literature as well as original documents regarding the time period when the lighthouse was active were searched then professional decorators were consulted. F. Ross Holland, a National Park Service authority on lighthouses reported:

> The lighthouse is ... large, especially for a lighthouse with a 5th Order lens. Many other more prominently sited lighthouses did not have such spacious quarters. The government simply did not provide elaborate living space for the keepers ... Normally lighthouses did not have both living rooms and parlors. Keepers [usually] just simply had the bare space necessary to exist and not always comfortably.

The kitchen was not large enough to eat in so it was decided to turn it into a working kitchen and convert the room directly in front of it into the dining room. The other room in the front of the structure was designated as the parlor. There were 4 bedrooms upstairs. It is not known if the oil butts (wooden barrels) were kept in the oil room as indicated on the house plans or in the basement.

At any rate, lists were made and furnishings were collected from wherever they could be located and placed in the appropriate rooms.

It was decided to furnish only two of the upstairs bedrooms. One is called the "parents room" and the other the "children's room".

The largest room was dedicated to the US Life Saving Service and the Coast Guard. The other small room, presently in

Shutters open – shutters closed.

restoration, will become a sewing room and guest room (for the lighthouse inspector.)

After everything was in place, a Park Aide opened the building for selected hours, only a few days a week. It was thought that the lighthouse would not need to be opened in the winter. The committee also decided it should not be lived in. Sometimes when visitors to the park drove by, it looked empty and forlorn, even though it was a beautiful building once again.

Finally, in 1988, a group was formed that would keep the lighthouse open to the public on a daily basis in the summer and week-ends in the winter. To this writing, those of us who work there hear people say, "It was always closed when we have come here before".

Not any more!

The lighthouse is open to the public daily starting with the Memorial Day weekend through September 30. The hours are 11:00 a.m. - 5:00 p.m.

During winter months, October 1 - Memorial Day, the light-house is open only weekends: 12:00 noon to 4:00 p.m. and for a special Hallloween party. In December, the lighthouse is open one weekend for a Holiday Open House celebration.

Weddings and special tours in the lighthouse can be arranged any time of the year but always by appointment. ◊

Seasonal lighting is provided by the Friends of the Lighthouse.

10. Enjoying the Flora

The lighthouse sits on a knoll in the middle of Yaquina Bay State Park which is at the north end of the bridge across Yaquina Bay. The view from the windows is of the busy river flowing under the bridge then emptying into the Pacific; fishing and pleasure boats coming and going; freighters inching their way into the harbor; whales feeding near the surf line; beachcombers finding treasures; fishermen balancing on the boulders of the jetty hoping for a "big one" and the often times wild Pacific Ocean ever washing against the beach and jetties.

All of these scenes are in the distance. What lies at the very doorstep of the lighthouse? We walked through the park with Don Giles, a scientist now retired from Oregon State University's Hatfield Marine Science Center in Newport. We learned:

Normally, when he takes a group for a nature walk, they start in the parking lot below the lighthouse and enjoy the downward view of the jetties. He askes folks to tell him, without looking, which side of the bridge behind them is higher. This is to get them to thinking about the geology of the area as the lighthouse is built on an uplifted marine terrace.

Many years ago, the area was a flat, sandy beach such as the beach below the lighthouse. But the sand has responded to the movements of the ocean floor thus, the lighthouse is built on a knoll about 60 to 80 feet high.

They discuss the jetties, which were the first ones built in the Pacific Northwest. The building specifications were for east coast jetty designs as the Corps of Engineers had no experience with the terrific winter storms along the Pacific Northwest coast. As we have seen, they quarried sandstone. Don exclaimed:

This was simply amazing. So they went over by Elk City* and bought it there. After it was installed in the jetty it was destroyed almost immediately. It was just not sturdy enough. The Corps had to redesign all of their specifications and now the jetty is made of basalt. The basalt may have come from around Detroit, Oregon in the Cascade Mountains. The last basalt on the extension of the south jetty and repair of the north jetty came from near Kelso, Washington.

---

* Elk City is upriver from Newport about 15 miles. Detroit is up the Santiam River canyon 52 miles east of Salem. The locals in Mill City have told us, 'Everyone up here knows the

Don goes on to tell about the beach sand:

In our part of the world, in the summer time, because of the prevailing winds and current, the sand travels south, and then in the winter, because of the storms coming out of the southwest, the sand goes north again. So, while millions of cubic yards of sand are moving, essentially it's a net of zero. But stick a jetty out there and you trap it.

Then we walk into the wooded part of the park to start the nature walk.

We find all three species of blackberries here; the native, or wild blackberry with three leaflets (*Rubus ursinus*) with one petiole and three smaller leaves and the two introduced from Europe; the Himalayan, (*Rubus procerus*) which has five leaves and is deciduous. The Evergreen (*Rubus laciniatus*) which also has five leaves but they're highly dissected.

Don thinks the Himalayan got its name from the fact that it makes such large, massive mounds like the mountain range of the same name. It will also interbreed with the evergreen thus we see some weird hybrids.

Other berries in the park are the Evergreen (*Vaccinium ovatum*) and Red Huckleberry (*V parvifolium*). The Evergreen is identified by its shiny, evergreen leaves and its small, dark blue berries. The Red grows rather tall and has leathery, serrated leaves with dark red berries. Another nearby park has two more varieties of Huckleberries: the Fool's (*Menziesia ferruginea*) and Bog (*Vaccinium uliginosum*). The flowers look like creamy little round bells.

Another delicious berry in the park near the lighthouse is the deciduous Thimbleberry (*Rubus parviflorus*).When it is ripe, it looks just like a red raspberry only it has a slightly "wild" taste. There is a wonderful patch along the road leading off Highway 101 into the park. The stalks are particularly thorny and the leaves are lobed (maple-like).

Speaking of Thimbleberry leaves, Don tells this story:

These leaves are sometimes referred to as "Logger's toilet paper, for these leaves are very soft. One time a mom and her two children were along on a nature walk and heard me refer to it by it's nickname. Her little girl on a later camping trip found a patch of Thimbleberries and ate quite a lot. This

rock for the jetties came from Hogg Rock.' The rock is about 1 mile west of the summit of the Cascades 4,817-feet elevation. It was named for Colonel T. Egenton Hogg who was the promoter of the Yaquina railroad.

frightened the mom, since she couldn't remember if the berries were toxic or not, so she took the girl to the hospital at Lincoln City. All she could remember was 'Logger's toilet paper.'

Of course, no one at the hospital had ever heard of that nor had the people at the Portland Poison Control Center. Someone suggested they call me. I was able to assure them everything would be fine. The girl had just eaten some very delicious native Oregon berries.

Twinberry (*Lonicera involucrata*) is also found in the park in abundance. The yellow flowers bloom early in the spring and when the berries set on, they are surrounded by bright red leaves. They are not poisonous but are not tasty at all. But the birds eat them.

Don Giles points out the one Red Flowering Currant (*Ribes sanguineum*) in the park. Its flowers come out before the leaves. The leaves are tiny, delicate and bright green and the berries hang thick along the stalks.

Of course there is the long-stemmed Salmonberry (*Rubus Spectablis*). This is thimble-shaped and is like a salmon-colored raspberry. Don tells us we can impress people when we point to these in winter. "Well, how do you know? You know because you were there when it was in flower and it had the leaves on it."

The giant Sitka spruce (*Picea sitchensis*) tree in the picnic area is, in Don's words:

...magnificent! I'd like to know how old that tree is. Probably 250 years. But it's obviously undergone a lot of trauma in its life. It's really highly branched. In the woods when you have these massive branches coming off like these they are actually weak areas the loggers call 'widow makers.' I wouldn't be out in a high wind right here, but it's a magnificent tree. It's like the Octopus Tree at Cape Meares, 70-some miles up the coast.*

---

* Spruce was logged shortly after the turn of the century. There were many labor strikes in the woods and in the mills then the government stepped in. They needed the spruce for lumber in making aircraft for the First World War so they put together the "Spruce Battalion" of the Signal Corps. What many years later would become the U. S. Air Force was the Air Service branch of the Signal Corps That was because aircraft were used for observation work – spotting where artillery shells were landing – as well as for pursuit planes – chasing and shooting down German planes. For spruce, they logged all over Lincoln County and built a mill in Toledo which is now the GP mill. However, the Armistice was signed November 11, 1918 before a single stick of lumber was made.

South of Waldport, about 5 or 6 miles, is a road leading to Camp 1, where one can see the old railroad right of way into the spruce forests, and up near Siletz is Camp 12, two of the old logging camps left from this endeavor.

The Shore Pine (*Pinus contoria* var. *contorts*) is interesting because people from Eastern Oregon and Eastern Washington, or at least those who know that area, know the same species of trees as Lodge pole Pine (*Pinus contoria* var. *latifolia*). Giles points out:

Books tell us that if the tree is small or shrubby and it grows near sea level it is Shore Pine. If the tree is larger, or if it grows inland above 3,000 feet elevation, it is Lodge pole Pine. Their cones and needles look alike.

Don continues:

Another thing that people seem to be interested in is the sculpturing of vegetation and the true story here is 'salt cropping.' It works this way: The winds blowing over the ocean pick up water droplets and each water droplet has a nucleus of salt. On the windward side, or in this case the ocean side, the water falls onto the trees, the water evaporates, leaving the salt behind. The salt then draws moisture from the plant at the growing points and that, then, stunts the growth. Then, while a lot of people say it is 'wind-blown,' the wind is the <u>vector</u>, like the mosquito is the <u>vector</u> for malaria, but it is actually the salt – 'salt-blown' – from the ocean."

Don Giles then mentioned the growth of the pines:

These shore pines are two year pines. Year zero, a little purple cone is starting. In May, yellow pollen covers the ground from the male cones. The second year cones release the seeds. You can show visitors this as you study the limbs. Take them down to the limb and see this year's cone, last year's cone and 3 to 4 years ago. You can appreciate how fast these trees are growing.

We didn't discuss the birds in the park at any length and nothing about the little animals we see around here.

Sometimes there are Brown Pelicans down there in the bay (as well as seals). Western gulls are the largest gull here with white head, yellow bill, red spot on lower bill, light gray wings, black wing tips and pink feet. The other gull that is closely related is the glaucous-winged gull (which means gray, but people don't like that complicated word). It is identical to the Western, but it does not have black wing tips. "It takes about four years for them to become sexually mature. A lot of people think that the brown and gray gulls are females but there is no difference between the sexes except for a small size difference. When people ask how to tell the sexes apart, I say, 'Why do you want to know? As long as the gulls know, that's what counts! If you see two gulls, side by side, fully adult, fully mature, and they have typical gull colors and one has a larger head, it is a male.

So now we know about seagulls. (Just remember to wear a hat when in "seagull country.")

There are many other birds in the park such as robins, ravens woodpeckers and hummingbirds. Don left us laughing with the story of a bird watcher on the annual Christmas Bird count who logged a "Blue Magpie." The *Blue Magpie* is a ship that sank at the end of the north jetty in 1983 and its remains were still visible at the time.*

Don Giles related that:

Scotch broom (*Cytisis scoparius*) was introduced here for dune stabilization and like all pea plants, it is important because its root system has a series of nodules that have a bacteria that takes nitrogen from the air. For most living things, this nitrogen is inert and can't be used, but Scotch Broom changes it into nitrates and nitrites so, essentially, it fertilizes the ground for other things to come. Red alder does the same thing. It has the same kind of roots. A problem with Scotch Broom is that it has a high oil content and is a severe fire starter. Even worse, though is Gorse, 'Irish Furse' (*Ulex europaeus*) which is easier to recognize. It's sort of like Scotch Broom, ex-cept it's very prickly and a darker green. The town of Bandon on the South Oregon coast, was destroyed in the mid 1930s when a fire started in the Gorse, jumped the highway and burned everything within its range right to the beach. The Gorse is still prevalent on the south coast but now people are tearing a lot of it out down there.

Gorse Alert

Don Giles admonished if any Gorse is seen growing up here to call the Lincoln County Weed Control (503-265-5747) because Gorse, which grows in profusion near Bandon, a fire hazard, is not wanted in the Newport area.

Don talked about a horticultural variety of Scotch Broom called Moonlight Broom which grows near the bridge. This grows in a mound, not tall bushes and has a lighter colored flower. We have also noticed another variety along the light-house path which is yellow and red. These varieties are found in local nurseries.

We went into an area of the park where the dune grass is growing and learned more:

We introduced European Dune Grass (*Ammophila arenaria*) near the

---

* For photograph and details of the wreck of the 350-foot long *Blue Magpie* that broke into 3 sections during a sea that was running 15 to 25 feet, and the Coast Guard's rescue of the crew, refer to *Oregon's Seacoast Lighthouses.* See bibliography

turn of the century, and again in the late 1920's. European Dune Grass has round leaves and very sharp tips. The American (*El-vmus mollis*) is broad leafed and a slightly different greener color and tends to droop more." "This European stuff out-competes and it does a good job of beach stabilization. In some places people say it does too good a job. They want to remove it now so the sands will start moving. It was planted every 18-inches" and the roots go down as far as 30-feet, but it comes back after being covered with 6 to 7 feet of sand. If you look at the roots in a dune slide, you see very fine mesh rootlets.

He also spotted a sedge. We felt the base of the leaf and found it was triangular. All of this lush vegetation is a product of our wet and mild climate.

Walking down a path behind the lighthouse, Don mentions different plants. "Pacific Wax Myrtle or Pacific Bayberry (*My-ca California*) is not a myrtle, but it's called that. In fruit it has very waxy berries. There are some introduced plums or cherries here." There is also have a gnarled old apple tree hidden in one corner of the back yard.

"Beautiful rhododendrons here. I don't know how old they are, but their large size is not unusual for this area." He had earlier told us that huckleberries, rhododendrons, azalea, salal and kinnikinnick (*Arcostaph-vlos uva-ursi*) are in the same heath family, with the rhododendron and azalea being in a separate subfamily.

Salal (*Gaultheria shallon*) grows profusely here in the park. Its flowers and fruit are larger versions of the huckleberry. However, there is more of a wild taste to them. Your author has made some jam out of them just to see what it tasted like – delicious! One just has to be sure the berries aren't overripe, or they tend to get wormy. The greens are widely used by florists. In fact, there is quite a local industry supplying salal leaves to florists nationwide.

We have two kinds of fern in the park: Bracken (*Ptex-idium aquilinum*) and Common Sword Fern (*Polystichum munitum*).

False Lily of the Valley (*Maianthemum dilatatum*) grows well in this environment. It has a spike of white flowers and carpets the woods in some places. This plant is very common. It has three names: Douglas's Spirea, actually it's scientific name (*Spix-ea douglassi*). It is also called steeplebush or hardhack.

Compare this view of the flora with picture on page 60.

This bush is really a pretty rosy color when it's in full bloom. <u>It is a rose,</u> by the way.

Another plant that grows in abundance in the park is Holly, but it is not a native of the area.

One last glance out toward the jetties brought this reminder from Don Giles:

Stay away from the north jetty for safety's sake. There have been many tragedies, deaths and broken bones. No jetty is totally safe for walkers or fishermen but the south jetty is much more safe than the north. Those fishermen out there (on the north jetty) are taking their lives in their hands. There are different kinds of fish on either side of the jetties: flatfish on the ocean side, rockfish on the channel side. The fishing should be equally good off both jetties so there is no reason to go out on the north jetty. It is my view the north jetty should be closed to foot traffic.

He left us with a hearty laugh saying, "I don't do mushrooms. I don't even <u>see</u> them. Moss either."

When one comes to the park for a picnic or to visit the lighthouse, take a walk through it and think about the plants and animals that inhabit this special place. Don's message is that there is tremendous diversity out there. ◊

11. Guns at the Lighthouse

The first time we heard about guns in connection with the lighthouse was when Ray Wells told us about living there as a young teenager. It was during World War II when he said that his family were the only civilians allowed on "the hill" and that the place was "bristling with gun emplacements."

The National Guard office and museum at Clackamas, Oregon has no record relating to this. A guess was that if there was a gun up there it might have been something like a 155mm artillery gun that was mounted on a concrete circle so it could be rotated. If this is so, there is only one place for a gun of such nature so "bristling" would not be the right word. But the truth of the matter is there were no "155-pieces" ever there or anywhere else on the Oregon coast during World War II.

Bert Webber, in his book *Silent Siege-III** in the chapter dealing with the World War II Beach Patrol, points out that all the coast was patrolled 24-hours a day, rain or shine against the risk of Japanese invasion. The hill where the lighthouse was situated was an excellent lookout spot and the government "requisitioned" the lighthouse as a military need immediately after "the day of infamy" – Pearl Harbor Day, December 7, 1941.

There were Coast Guard lookouts stationed there with binoculars, a long-scope and 1903 Springfield .30 caliber rifles. These men also carried side-arms, usually .45 caliber Colt revolver in holsters on gun belts. Such a scene could surely be interpreted as "bristling with guns" to a young teenager.

The next time we learned of guns, was when the restoration

---

* *Silent Siege III: Japanese Attacks On North America in World War II; Ships Sunk, Air Raids, Bombs Dropped, Civilians Killed.* For a very detailed description of how the Beach Patrol Detachments were equipped and operated see: *Lakeport, Ghost Town of the South Oregon Coast.* See also *Oregon's Salty Coast* These are in the bibliography.

took place. It seems a revolver was found among the junk that had accumulated through the years. No one recalls the make, size, or what happened to it.

In July 1990 another gun was found. The park crew was building a new path up the side of the hill when they uncovered a hand gun a few inches under the soil. It was in extremely bad condition and parts fell from it as it was picked up.

A report was made to the local police and the gun was sent to the history section of the Oregon State Parks Department. Their first impression was that it was similar to a Smith & Wesson .32 or .38 caliber pistol. Detailed measurements and photographs were taken and the gun was carefully checked for potential hazard, or cartridge that might still be stuck, unseen, in the decayed mechanism.

During a final cleaning process, a seam was discovered on the gun's underside. The quality of metal appeared sub-standard for a gun but scrutiny with a jeweler's lens continued. Finally, a small trademark was discovered. The gun was determined to be from the Kilgore Toy Company made in 1935.

So much for guns at the lighthouse. ◊

12. Are There Ghosts in the Lighthouses?

> While there has always been public interest in visiting the lighthouse, when the Federal Writer's Project was created during the Great Depression years, their guide book (*Oregon, End of the Trail*) that finally appeared in 1940, declares, on page 376:
>
> ### Newport has a HAUNTED LIGHTHOUSE
>
> Almost immediately, people started flocking to the lighthouse to "check it out." Now that the lighthouse is an official Oregon State Park, the crowds are even greater 50 years later and the visitors are still asking about the ghosts.

There is probably not a lighthouse anywhere that does not have at least one cracker-jack of a ghost story. The Yaquina lighthouses are not exceptions.

Is it the ever-changing lights and shadows caused by the revolving beam in the tower that plays tricks with one's mind? Is it a gale-force blow that tears branches off trees and roars down chimneys that brings ghosts to mind? Maybe it's the fog as it creeps slowly over the ocean, over the beach and swirls about a lighthouse causing one to just dare to step out of the shelter of the warm cocoon of the lighthouse so it can wrap you in its cold, clammy blanket.

Perhaps your favorite lighthouse is not a warm and comfy place at all. Perhaps it is a damp, abandoned, totally impersonal relic of a lighthouse – almost like a prison in its appearance because of its remoteness out on a rock or at the edge of a headland all alone, far away from anywhere.

How do ghost stories come about? Someone, somewhere has to get one started probably by telling a tale of imagination. These stories seem to grow with every telling for the next person adds something and on and on and on. Good ghost stories have a reasonable chain of circumstances – at least parts of the facets are

Crowds wait for door to open on Halloween for a fun time at the lighthouse.

plausible – and often times they are pegged to a documented event. With enough telling and appearances in print, pretty soon many people are ready to believe we have a real ghost.

There is a story of a hitch-hiker during the 1970s that he bedded down one summer's night in front of the lighthouse. This was after eating a can of cold beans and swigging white wine from a jug. Later he recalled he saw the ghost and talked to her. In fact, she promised him that he would get a job the next day which he did.

When one of the lighthouse guests read that account his reaction was, "Humph—! After eating a can of beans and drinking a bottle of wine and probably smoking some of that "wacky tabaccy" he probably did see something not necessarily a ghost."

Police Hear Things.

Nov. 19, 1993 1:57 a.m.— Caller reported a perimeter floor sensor at the Yaquina Bay Lighthouse activated. An officer reported finding footprints leading to the front door but although no entry point was found sounds were coming from inside.
– *News-Times*. Newport, Ore.

The Moaning of Beautiful Zynna

A gentleman, from a ship of foreign registry that had stopped for fresh water in 1875, just a year after the Yaquina Bay Light-house closed, left his charge, the young Zynna, in the care of a Newport family. He paid them the money needed for her care until he would return. As Zynna advanced through her 'teen years she was described as "beautiful" by almost everyone who saw her. And she was very popular among her peers.

As she entered womanhood she fell in love with a handsome young man of this seaport town. One day, the couple joined other young people for a picnic at the deserted lighthouse. The group walked through the town and up the side of the steep hill to the lighthouse. After lunch they frolicked in the afternoon summer sunshine and some of them sojourned to the lighthouse. Late in the day when they were readying to leave, Zynna said to her lover that she must go back to the lighthouse to get her gloves. When she didn't return, he went to seek her but now found the lighthouse door locked and no Zynna in sight.

He called her name a number of times but she did not appear. Alarmed, he ran after the group, which was now about a quarter-of-a-mile away, seeking their help. On being advised that Zynna had disappeared, all of the group raced back to the lighthouse. Although the party split into pairs and searched all of the grounds until nightfall, no one was found. Sadly and without words, they made their way to their homes.

The next morning they, with several more of the townsfolk, returned. Some of the men broke down the door to the lighthouse. Then everyone made a room-by-room search. Two of the boys ascended the stairs into the tower but Zynna was not found anywhere in the lighthouse. However, a sudden shriek from the kitchen brought everyone running into that room. One of the girls had discovered a single large drop of blood on the floor. It was bright red. It looked very fresh.

Additional men from the village were summoned to thoroughly comb every inch of the lighthouse, its attic, all the ground all the way into town and down the face of the headland to the water. There was no sign of Zynna. In the days that followed, to everyone's amazement, the drop of blood remained bright and fresh! This phenomenon lasted for over three months. Then the blood spot just disappeared.

Originally, when the gentleman hired the services of the foster parents in Newport, he never revealed when he would return. And he didn't. No one remembered the name of his ship.

The beautiful Zynna was never found and no additional clues were ever discovered as to the cause of her disappearance.

After the U. S. Life Saving Service occupied the old lighthouse in the early 1900s, it was said that the men could not explain strange creakings of the floor, sighs and moans of a young woman's voice floating through the old building in the night.

On November 19, 1993, at 1:57 a.m. a report reached the Newport Police Department that a floor sensor at the lighthouse had been activated. A darkened prowl car arrived and the officer, cautiously looked around, found footprints leading up the steps to the front door. But the door was secure and there were no footprints going back down. Although there were no lights seen in the lighthouse, he reported there were sounds coming from inside.

Had Zynna come back?

—Bonaparte Franklin Tuleeke IV

*   *   *

"The Haunted Lighthouse" story has been a classic for decades and from time to time it appears, with various adaptations, in newspapers and in magazines – even in books. To omit it from a history of the lighthouse where it originated would be unseemly. As far as can be determined, the original story was written by Lischen M. Miller and published in the *Pacific Monthly* Vol. II, in 1899.

Mrs. Miller was the daughter of the pioneer Cogswell family of Eugene. The Miller/Cogswell house still stands on the side of Skinner's Butte. It is privately owned.

In a telephone interview with a great, great grand nephew of Mrs. Miller, it was found that she was cultural, artistic and especially noted for theatrical talents. But why did she choose Yaquina Bay Lighthouse as the setting for a ghost story?

Plausibly she visited Newport at a time when the old building looked its worst and the genesis of an idea was planted. The story is still popular and visitors to the lighthouse still expect to see a ghost.

The comments of some of today's visitors at the lighthouse about the ghost story are intriguing. One person stated emphatically that her mother remembers when the "lighthouse keeper's daughter was murdered." But the descendants of the keeper also very emphatically declare that none of the keeper's children were murdered. Judging from the approximate age of the lady who remembered this, her mother could not have been living at the time of the alleged "ghost story."

Another "recollection" is that when a woman was a little girl, her horseback riding instructor from Toledo had been in the search party that had "hunted for the young girl who disappeared in the lighthouse." Again, this lady was not old enough to have had an instructor in her childhood that could have participated in the search for the girl.

As it seems to be impossible to get rid of the lighthouse ghost, try this one:

"Lighthouse hosts should be there to great the public and help make their visit a pleasant one." This was part of the orientation park volunteers received.

The day had been fairly busy. Several hundreds of visitors had wandered through and a lull in the activity was welcome. The weather had been pleasant with bright, warm sunshine and a gentle off-shore breeze. Then, within minutes, fog had thrown a clammy blanket about the trees and wrapped the lighthouse closely in its folds. It became eerie — ghostly.

I sat down, leaned my head back and closed my eyes but just for a minute.

The gentle scent of roses wafted through the room. My eyes seemed glued shut but I could "see" the apparition that drifted toward me. It was like looking through a negative against a bright light. My throat seemed paralyzed yet my mind was working.

"So! You're the one that goes around saying there isn't any ghost; that it's just a story. Huh! Just a story, indeed"!

"OK," my mind said, "tell me what really happened."

"Not yet! Can you imagine what it's been like around here all these years? People blaming me for mysterious lights and even saying they've *seen* me? Giving me credit for finding jobs for them. Saying I'm sealed in a brick wall, or in a cistern, or I'm still roaming around her at night? Everyone is scared of me. But the most disgusting thing of all is sharing this place with that crusty old sea captain. He's no fun to have around. Spends most of his time in the cellar talking to himself and smoking his stinking old pipe."

"You've got to admit the place looked haunted for a long time. And people do talk, you know."

"Yes but that isn't my fault. It wasn't so bad when those men lived here. They were too tired from working on the jetty or rescuing shipwrecked sailors to pay any attention to me. But when they restored this place and found the gun they almost found out what really happened.

"Are you ready to tell me"?

"I guess after all these years someone should know."

"I'm not sure I want the responsibility of being the only one to know. Who would believe me"?

"That's your problem. You see, when I went back upstairs to get my handkerchief, there was a blinding flash, a loud noise and...."

As she spoke these words, the sun broke through the fog, footsteps thundered up the front steps, the front door opened and we had visitors again. Their first question was "Is the ghost story <u>really</u> true?

"OOOoOhhhhh Nooooooo.... My voice trailed off into silence. I was standing in an invisible cloud of rose-scent.

"ʏʏʏʏYYYe-Yesssssssssssss," I corrected stammering, "It could very well be true."

The scent of roses faded away, then a chilling laugh seemed to float down the stairwell. Our guests froze. Their eyes became enlarged with apprehension. I glanced out of the window and saw that the wind had come up and was pushing the fog back in around the lighthouse.

"Don't be frightened," I admonished, "It is only the wind howling down the chimney."

But the guests turned away, raced out of the door and down the steps....

—Dorothy Wall

*　　　　*　　　　*

The Haunted Lighthouse

Situated on the Oregon coast, at the entrance to Yaquina Bay, is an old deserted lighthouse. Its weather-beaten walls are wrapped in mystery. Of an afternoon when the fog comes drifting in, it can be the loneliest place in the world. At times those who chance to be in the vicinity hear a moaning sound like the cry of one in pain, and sometimes a frenzied call for help pierces the deathlike stillness of the waning day. At times a light gleams from the lantern tower where no lamps are ever trimmed.

In the days when Newport was but a handful of cabins, across the bar there sailed a sloop grotesquely rigged and without a name. Her skipper appeared as a beetle-browed ruffian with a scar across his cheek from mouth to ear. From the ship a boat was lowered and in it was a tall man about forty years of age and a young girl. The oarsmen rowed them to the landing. Ashore, the man explained that the ship had encountered rough weather and his daughter found the voyage very difficult. He said if a place could be found for her to stay, he wished to leave her in the village while he finished some business in another port then he would be back to get her in about two weeks.

A place was found so the man sent the boatmen back to the sloop for her trunk. When the sailors got back to the landing they carried the girl's trunk to a nearby house. Muriel Trevenard, as was her name, was a delicate-looking, fair-haired girl still in her teens. She spent many hours each day with a sketch book and pencil in that grassy hollow in the hill. The fortnight lengthened to a month but there was no sign of the sloop.

It was in August that a group of vacationers hiked over the Coast Range and came into the village. They were not long in discovering Muriel. She joined them in their ceaseless excursions and quickly became one of the group.

The Cape Foulweather lighthouse, just 3 miles away, had just been completed so the lighthouse upon the bluff above Newport was now deserted. Some member of the camping party proposed that they hike up to the old lighthouse and look around. With much merry talk and laughter, they climbed the hill. Harold Welch unlocked the door and they went into the empty hall that echoed dismally to the sound of human voices. Stairs led up to a small landing from which a little room, probably a linen closet, opened. It was well furnished but from its only unoccupied wall dangled a length of wainscoting.

"Why," cried one, "this house seems to be falling to pieces. "He pulled at a section and it easily came away. Behind was a heavy piece of sheet iron. He also pulled on this and when it moved to one side, a number of the visitors peered into the aperture. It went straight back then dropped abruptly into a soundless well. "Who knows what it is"?

"Smugglers," suggested somebody, and they all laughed. But everyone seemed strangely nervous as well as excited. There seemed to be something uncanny in the atmosphere that oppressed them with an unaccountable sense of dread. Feeling they had seen enough, they descended the stairs having left the dark closet open. Everyone hurried out of the lighthouse into the thickening gray fog.

Harold Welch stopped to lock the door but Muriel laid her hand on his arm and declared: "I must go back. I must have dropped my handkerchief upstairs."

Perhaps because her slightest wish was beginning to be his law of life, he reluctantly let her go. She started up the steps and he joined the others. He had just caught up with the stragglers of the party when the somber stillness of the darkening day was rent by a shriek so wild and weird that all who heard it felt their blood freeze in their veins.

"Muriel, we are coming" they shouted. "Don't be afraid!" But there was no reply. In only seconds all were streaming into the lighthouse then up the stairs and there, on the floor, they were horrified as they stared at a pool of warm, red blood. There were blood drops in the hall and on the landing. In the linen closet they picked up a blood-stained handkerchief. But there was nothing else. They saw that the iron door had been replaced and the panel in the wainscot was closed. But try as they might, none of them could pry open that door.

Back in the village the group went to where Muriel lived and told the strange story. "This will be a dreadful blow to her father," remarked the housekeeper. I don't want to be the one to have to break it to him."

And she had her wish. Neither the sloop nor Muriel's father ever again sailed into Yaquina Bay.

—Adapted from Lischen Cogswell Miller (1858-1915)*

---

* Mrs. Miller was the sister-in-law of poet Joaquin Miller because she was married to his brother George. According to the family, she was a very dramatic person. When writing, when one word would do she used several. She had a great sense of imagination and probably wrote the ghost story as a fun thing. Others have embellished it therefore it has grown until it has become "absolute truth."

Yaquina Head Lighthouse viewed from short beach south of the head.

A theme upon which one might concoct a doozey of a ghost story could be based on a short sketch found in Gibb's book, *Oregon's Seacoast Lighthouses*: A persistent rumor for years has been that a workman fell into the hollow, between the double walls, of the Yaquina Head Lighthouse tower while it was being built. As there was no way to retrieve the body other than tearing out a part of the tower, it was left entombed and eventually sealed in what became a walled crypt. While this yarn has never been proven it's still told today, especially when the weather is dark, cold and foggy. It is said that if one stands in the top of the tower one might hear the ghost climbing the 144 circular iron stairs behind him.

*   *   *

The Ghostly Keeper At
Yaquina Head Lighthouse

(Author's note: Some time ago a young boy of 8 years, and his parents, came to see us at the Light House. The boy said he was sorry that Yaquina Head Lighthouse did not have a ghost story so he wrote one. His mom helped him with it.)

Through the years, visitors to and caretakers of the Yaquina Head Lighthouse have reported seeing strange and unusual occurrences. Especially on stormy and foggy nights, some have heard an eerie, sad and hollow sounding voice coming from the lighthouse tower. This is the story of when these strange sight-ings began.

In 1898, James Miller was the captain of a fishing boat named *The Ocean Princess*. Captain Miller had named his boat after his small daughter, whom he affectionately called "Princess". The captain was an experienced seaman and a successful fisherman who made a good living and kept his family well-fed with the fishes and crabs he brought home.

Each day Captain Miller's little daughter would anxiously wait for him to come home. She would give him a big hug and bring him his slippers and his pipe and snuggle up on his lap as soon as he was seated in his favorite chair.

One night "Princess" waited and waited, but Captain Miller did not come home. The fog and rain had become very thick that afternoon. The wind howled and by evening, it was impossible to see even a few feet. The sea was very rough and furious waves pounded against the rocks.

Out on the *Ocean Princess* Captain Miller fought to bring his ship to the shore. Large rocks loomed up out of the fog as he tried to see his way. Suddenly, a huge wave more than 20 feet high swept him off-board. He struggled to swim in the rough, icy water. He couldn't see in the thick fog. But finally, he saw a small glimmer of light. Judging from where he thought his position was when he was swept off the boat, Captain Miller knew this light was the beacon of the Yaquina Head Lighthouse. He swam with all his might toward the light fighting the rough waves and strong current and cold water. He wondered how long his strength would hold out and he concentrated on that distant light.

The next morning the ship could be seen in the bay drifting aimlessly. When a crew went to check the ship, they found it deserted. They recognized the *Ocean Princess* as belonging to Captain Miller. On the shore near the lighthouse, they found a hat and several pieces of clothing but never found a body. The searchers were despondent as they went to Captain Miller's home to report what they had found. Captain Miller's daughter, "Princess" was so heartbroken that she stopped talking for a long time. Everyday she would sadly walk down to the lighthouse and sit silently crying and looking out to sea. Although she finally did recover enough to talk, she never was the same again and she never stopped her vigil at the lighthouse everyday until she died. Some people said she met her father there each night as she had done at home but no one ever knew for sure. Some townspeople said they had seen her off in the distance sitting on a rock and talking and laughing with a tall, weathered-looking man in a captain's hat. But, they were not certain because a minute later she would be sitting silently alone, as usual.

Beginning the very night after the clothing was found near the lighthouse, the lighthouse keeper reported unusual events at the lighthouse. Often at night as he sat alone at his post watching the lighthouse lamp, he would notice that doors would seem to open or close by themselves. On a few occasions, he caught a glimpse of a man standing on the stairway up to the lighthouse tower. When he would look closer or take a step to investigate, the man would disappear.

The keeper not only saw strange things, but also began to hear someone calling in a kind of moaning and hollow-sounding voice. It sounded as if the voice was saying something like: "Princess, my Princess. Come to me." When the keeper told people about it they wouldn't believe him. They told him it must only be the wind. But behind his back, people would say the keeper must be going crazy. Eventually, some visitors to the lighthouse began to report hearing and seeing strange things too. And these occurrences continued for many, many years, long after the first lighthouse keeper had been replaced and many keepers had come and gone. Reports of strange happenings and sightings have continued even to the present time.

About 60 years after Captain Miller's disappearance, the lighthouse keeper reported seeing a figure of a man standing by the huge lamp and staring out to sea. The keeper stood and watched this figure for about five minutes and the pale-looking man just stood motionless looking out to sea. The keeper said the man looked very sad and his clothes were torn and weathered. When the keeper tried to speak to the man, the man turned slightly and looked at the keeper and then slowly faded away. This same lighthouse keeper also told how sometimes he would hear footsteps in the hall or sometimes he would have the sensation of someone looking over his shoulder as he read, but when he would turn around, no one was there.

Even to this day, especially at night in foul weather, the figure of a man wearing a captain's hat has been seen in the doorway or window of the lighthouse. The lighthouse keeper, as well as some local residents who have also seen the figure, identified the image from old family photographs in the possession of his daughter's descendants, as old Captain Miller.

—Jesse Bjornsen

Are there ghosts in the lighthouses? You are invited to investigate. If you dare!◊

In 1950, Colleen Moynahan and her mother, Agnes, made the dress that Colleen wore for her marriage to Donald Angus McLean. The style then was to wear a full skirt. In 1993, forty-three years later, Colleen's youngest daughter Kate was married to Tony Vasquez in the historic old lighthgouse where Kate's great-great-great grandfather, Charles Peirce ,had been the lightkeeper.

She is also the namesake of the youngest of Charles and Sarah Peirce's brood. That earlier Kate was born in the lighthouse.

Since the lighthouse is an 1870's structure, Kate wanted an 1870's style dress therefore she and her mother reconstructed the dress and made a slim skirt of the earlier full skirt retaining the original tunic (top) as it was.

13. Weddings at the Lighthouse

While there were undoubtedly many weddings at the light-house over the decades, there does not seem to have been a formal list kept of them until recent years. A permit was issued in June of 1986 for a wedding that occurred on July 5th of that year. At that time the weddings were to be in the yard or on the front porch. A couple from Albany, Oregon chose the porch. Provisions, in effect at that time, required a written permit from the Oregon State Parks Division. Among the regulations were these:

In the event of rain, the wedding will be allowed to take place inside the Lighthouse. Each guest will be required to pay .50¢ entrance fee. No food or beverages will be allowed within and attendance will be limited to thirty people.

In recent years the restrictions have been modified considerably.

In 1989, a couple from Portland chose the lighthouse for their wedding setting. This was in July and the ceremony was in the

96

front yard. After that wedding we started to advertise that weddings could be held in or around the lighthouse. From then to the present time, there have been about sixty weddings. These were people from the Pacific Northwest states of Oregon, Washington and Idaho as well as from many others including Colorado, Missouri, Kentucky, Wisconsin and Canada. ◊

(Left page) Bride waits at head of steps for signal to come down for her wedding in the lighthouse. Stairs in back go to watchroom and tower. (This page) Dressed mannequins put action into the exhibits.

(Top) Refurbished
kitchen with pump.
(Lower) Antique reed
organ and many
other furnishings
have been collected
by Friends of the
Lighthouse as none
of the original
remain.

14. Friends of Yaquina Bay Lighthouse

Because it was difficult for the State Parks Department to obtain funding for rehabilitation of interpretive projects, a group of interested citizens, feeling that perhaps it might do better, called a meeting on July 13, 1988 to organize the Friends of Yaquina Bay Lighthouse.

One week later, a board of directors was elected and bylaws were adopted. At the same time, it was decided to design a brochure about the history of the lighthouse and the family that lived there as lighthouse keepers.

Until the Friends group was formed, there was an admittance fee for going through the building. Now, the fee could be discontinued with the Friends depending entirely on donations and gift shop sales to meet expenses. The Friends, being a Non-Profit Organization, could now apply for grants for various projects.

Volunteers of the Friends, augmented by selected towns-people as well as State Park volunteer hosts, staff the lighthouse.

When the Friends assumed "command" of the lighthouse, there was no place for a gift shop since each room had been furnished with exhibits. But the basement was warm and dry. It was cleaned, appropriately partitioned and lighted. This provided 3 rooms. The largest would became the gift shop. The other rooms became a stock room while the 3rd was turned into a video room.

The Friends group produced its own video – short history of the surrounding area and tour of the lighthouse that ends with a ghost story. This tape runs continuously when the lighthouse is open.

The gift shop features hats, "T" shirts and sweat shirts, all with the lighthouse emblazoned across the front. There are also books about the area. In addition is a wide variety of post cards, coloring books for the younger set, small models of the lighthouse, quilt blocks, posters and many other items all with a

Seasonal decoration and
visiting harpist.

Ornaments on the tree are hand-made. Note re-opened fireplace.

nautical theme.

The lighthouse is a special point of interest for large crowds on Halloween night when there is a special " showing" of the ghost and other spooky items. There are two open house celebrations during the year: One in early August. The other is during the first weekend of December when the house is decorated in a Victorian-looking holiday theme including strolling carolers amd other musicians.

The Friends constructed an informational kiosk near the parking lot and are working with Oregon State Parks to construct a handicap-accessible overlook off the parking lot. The view will include the historic bridge, the jetties and, of course, will look down on the river with it's constant parade of vessels.

Although the Friends group is small, it is ambitious and has positive goals. New members are welcome. For information and

| Yaquina Bay Lighthouse |
| Telephones: |
| 503/867-7451 |
| 505/265-5679 |

fees for weddings and private tours write to Friends of Yaquina Bay Lighthouse 846 SW Government St. Newport, Or 97365. ◊

—Photograph made in 1992.

15. Yaquina Head Lighthouse

For many years, decades in fact, there has been confusion about this lighthouse because many have declared that it was built in the wrong place. This stems from misplacing of names on early maps. Some say that when the ship with the building materials arrived, it obviously could not off-loaded on to the high bluffs of Cape Foulweather so an easier spot had to be found – Yaquina Head. This was 7 miles south of the cape and that was where the lighthouse was built – at the wrong place. Whoops!

James A. Gibbs* wrote:

This excellent folklore is extinguished by the most reliable source of all, George Davidson's 1889 *Pacific Coast Pilot*. He wrote: "In the published list of the Light-House Board this light [Yaquina] is designated Cape Foulweather [Yaquina Head]." Thus it was carried in the early lists as Cape Foulweather but in the 1896 *Light List* dropped the Cape Foulweather and henceforth utilized only Yaquina Head as the designation. Davidson, with the U.S. Coast & Geodetic Survey, was an expert in his field and gives a complete description of every detail of the Yaquina area as well as every other maritime geography and topography of the Pacific Coast.

---

* For an excellent account refer to Gibbs' *Oregon Seacoast Lighthouses*. See bibliography.

103

At 93-feet high, Yaquina Head Lighthouse is tallest lighthouse on Oregon coast. Only higher tower on the coast is the Astor Column in Astoria at 125-feet. (Inset) Year block "1872" is over the door.

Tidepool occupants can be viewed at low tide south of lighthouse.

Yaquina Head Lighthouse is at the end of a winding road that leaves Highway 101 at Agate Beach just north of Newport. For many years, the Head was the site of a large, privately owned gravel quarry that had to be crossed to get to the lighthouse. In a major land reclamation project, the Bureau of Land Management, Department of the Interior, has rehabilitated the area and constucted a modern access road.

(Top) Aerial view of Yaquina Head and its lighthouse photographed in May 1970 by Coast Guard. (Lower) Coast Guard reservation with lighthouse photographed in August 1956 by Bert Webber.

106

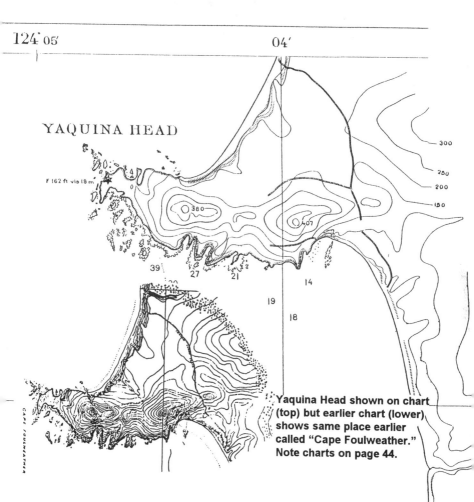

YAQUINA HEAD

F 162 ft vis 18 m

Yaquina Head shown on chart (top) but earlier chart (lower) shows same place earlier called "Cape Foulweather." Note charts on page 44.

Historically, the lighthouse reservation of 19.35 acres, contained residence quarters for the keepers, workshops and garages. In later years, after Coast Guard occupation, barracks were constructed as well as tall radio transmitter masts. After the lighthouse was automated, all of the buildings were dismantled, then removed, and the grounds thoroughly cleaned and planted. Gibbs wrote:

The tower (162-feet above the ocean beach) stands today in all its splendor, one of the Pacific Coast's finest towering lights. This lighthouse is a daily destination for scores of visitors who also take in surrounding grounds and beaches. The lighthouse reservation, managed by the B.L.M. is a mecca for viewing the sea bird refuge and the variety of sea life along the shore and at sea.

The lighting apparatus in Yaquina Head Lighthouse. Photo made in 1989.

This is a fixed-position lens that was first lighted on August 20, 1873 and is the tallest of all Oregon lighthouses. The light is 93 feet above the water. It was originally an oil lamp but was eventually converted to electricity. For many years the light source was a 1,000 watt T-12 motion picture projector lamp. The lighthouse was automated on May 1, 1966 and personnel transferred elsewhere. At the present time, the original 1st Order lens is in place but is illuminated with a 1,000 watt quartz iodine globe that generates approximately 131,000 candlepower. The light can be seen to about 19 miles in clear weather. The light operates 24-hours a day.

In an arrangement with the Coast Guard, which owns and operates the lighthouse, the B.L.M. has opened the reservation for visitors and at this writing expects to have the lighthouse also open shortly. The grounds are a wilflife sancturary.

This is a brick tower covered with stucco. The bricks came from San Francisco. The metal for the tower is from Philadelphia. Landing the materials and putting up the tower were mean jobs. Just getting supplies from the transporting vessel to the rock required lightering – use of a small boat or barge to deliver goods from a larger ship unable to navigate in shallow or close in-shore water – then hoisting the materials from the lighter to the top of the bluff. But to get from the top to the water required lengthy work chiseling steps out of the solid rock face.

Weather conditions had to be closely observed for if a rough sea was running, there would be no unloading that day. While there were no deaths* in the unloading process or in the construction of the lighthouse, there were some personal injuries.

Once when two lighters foundered, their cargoes were lost. This meant much delay while the ship went back, got more supplies then headed back to the Oregon coast. There was one incident that damaged the great 1st Order lens as it was being unloaded. Of course it had to be replaced. These incidents cost a lot of time loss as transportation was very slow.

Nevertheless, there was progress on the project with the workers laboring 10 to 12 hours every day including weekends. Putting up the tower was only one part of the job. This would be a residence-lighthouse therefore living quarters had to be constructed not just for the keeper but for the assistant keeper. Two-story frame buildings, heavily put together because of severe winds were constructed. And there were out-buildings. Oil for the beacon was kept in a separate building away from others due to constant fire hazard. For fresh water there was a cistern. Of course there was no electricity, no telephones, no radios (no television!), no running water so there were no inside bathrooms. This was still the era of Saturday night baths in a tub on the kitchen floor.

But the duty as a light keeper was good duty especially in the west. Wages were high compared to salaries for the same work on the Atlantic coast.

The new lighthouse became such an attraction to the locals and tourists, it was hard for the keepers and crew to get their work done. They asked the lighthouse board to establish visiting

---

* Building of coastal lighthouses can be hazardous to one's health. To enjoy the shear drama of precariously holding on to bare rock in a severe storm with no escape possible, refer to *Terrible Tilly; Tillamook Rock Lighthouse, an Oregon Documentary*. See bibliography.

Rocks at Yaquina Head Lighthouse Reservation is Wildlife refuge.

hours so the keepers and crew could get some sleep. They were averaging only about 5 hours of sleep at a time.

Because of the foggy, windy and rainy weather and the isolation of the station, it became very lonely for the wives. They found out that on wash day it was a good thing to hang the sheets out early before the winds came up or they would be ripped to shreds A school for the children was established in 1874 and was conducted in the "office" of the Ocean House Lodge in nearby Yaquina Bay owned by Samuel Case. Mr. Case was a former soldier from the Siletz garrison. He and his family were living at Ocean House at this time. The teachers were Miss Emily Stevens and Miss Hattie Wass. The school lasted until 1886.

Families raised vegetables, tended to the chickens and stock, fished, hunted and dug clams.

The first Keeper at Yaquina Head was Fayette S. Crosby who opened the lighthouse on August 20, 1873 and was there until December 23, 1875.

In August of 1888, a *female* assistant light keeper became a reality. She was Malinda J. Plummer, the wife of Keeper Frank Plummer.

110

Post Offices

One thing the keepers and their families wanted and had available to them was mail service. The Newport post office (opened July 2, 1868) was within walking distance of Yaquina Bay Lighthouse. The keepers at Yaquina Head Lighthouse were served by the same postoffice until April 18, 1912 when a new postoffice was opened at Agate Beach, three miles closer.

As the lighthouse was close to the ocean, it was struck many times by raging winter storms. When damage occurred, it would be months before major repairs could be made as approval had to come from the Light-House Board in Washington, D.C.

For many years there were no visitors permitted in the lighthouse and the tower was kept locked. Now that the Bureau of Land Management is maintaining and modernizing the old lighthouse reservation, visitors are expected once again to be able to climb the stairs to the tower starting in summer 1994. ◊

Appendix A
Oregon's Lighthouses
In the Order When Built
* Presently operating

1857*   **Umpqua River Lighthouse** (flashes red/white)
              No. 1 Destroyed in flood
              No. 2 Built 1894

1866*   **Cape Arago Lighthouse** (flashes white)
              No. 1 Destroyed by erosion
              No. 2 Built 1908 – Destroyed by erosion
              No. 3 Built 1934

1870*   **Cape Blanco Lighthouse** (flashes white)
              →Oldest continuously operating lighthouse in Oregon

1871 - 1874   **Yaquina Bay Lighthouse** (was fixed white)
              →Oregon's shortest-lived lighthouse. Now State Park

1873*   **Yaquina Head Lighthouse** (flashes white)

1875 - 1899   **Point Adams Lighthouse** (was fixed red)
              Dismantled 1912

1881 - 1957   **Tillamook Rock Lighthouse** (was white flash)
              Privately owned. Is Columbarium
              No trespassing – Federal wildlife refuge

1888*   **Warrior Rock Lighthouse** (flashes white)
              No. 1 Destroyed by flood
              No. 2 Built 1930. Destroyed by barge in 1969
              No. 3 Foundation repaired. No building – light and
              fog signal only. On Sauvie Island

1890 - 1958   **Cape Meares Lighthouse** (flashes white)
              Present light is airport-type beacon

1894*   **Heceta Head Lighthouse** (flashes white)
              Operated by Coast Guard but property transferred to Oregon
              State Parks on April 2, 1994

1895 - 1935   **Willamette River Lighthouse** (was white flash)

1896 - 1939   **Coquille River Lighthouse** (was white flash)
              Now part of Bullard's Beach State Park

1902 - 1964   **Desdemona Sands Lighthouse** (was white flash)

1976*   **Cleft of the Rock Lighthouse** (flashes red/white)
              Private ownership and operation – closed to visitors

112

Appendix B
A Plea For Clemency
The Court Martial of Captain C. H. Peirce

To His Excellency

U. S. Grant
President of U.S.A.
Washington, D.C.

Fort Tongass, Alaska Territory
December 1st, 1869

Mr. President

By the advice of the presiding officer of a General Court Martial, before which I have recently been tried and, feeling conscious of my innocence of any intentional fault of conduct, and having been in the service nearly twenty-four years, I am induced to lay my case before you earnestly requesting that such clemency may be extended to me as in your judgment my services would justify.

I am accused of being intoxicated three times in twenty months, on the 4th day of July and Christmas of 1868, and on the 23rd day of June 1869. Ref. the first two charges, I can declare that I am innocent. For what occurred on the 23rd of June, while in command of the post, I have thrown myself upon the mercy of the court. That I drank one glass of liquor, and one glass only, which rendered me unconscious for a brief period, I cannot deny.

I am charged with accusing an officer of my command of embezzling public funds. Of this charge I can also declare myself innocent, the witnesses for the prosecution and defense denying that any such words were spoken. The length of time which has elapsed since the alleged commission of the offenses has deprived me of several key witnesses, with whom I was obliged to hold intercourse on the different occasions when it is alleged that I was intoxicated. In consequence of their discharge from the service, I have been deprived of the benefit of their testimony.

If long and faithful service without a charge ever having, until now, been preferred against me entitles me to any consideration, I think I may partly claim it.

In June 1846, I entered the service at the age of seventeen, in the U. S. Engineer Troops, then just organized, and stationed at West Point. Was shortly afterwards ordered to the Rio Grande. Was one of the pioneers during march of Generals Patterson and Twiggs from Matamoros to Tampico, Mexico. Was engaged in the trenches during the entire siege of Vera Cruz. Took part in the battles of Cerro-Gordo, Contreras, Cherubusco, Chapultepec, Garita de Belen and two days in the City of Mexico. Was recommended for a Certificate of Merit for the battles of Contreras, Cherubusco and the City of Mexico. Was also honorably mentioned in the Official Reports of Commanding Officers now embodied in Senate documents. The youngest of my company, I was promoted to the rank of non-commissioned officer, shortly after entering the City of Mexico.

Upon the return of my company to West Point, N.Y. in 1849, was discharged. Re-enlisted and, upon the day of joining, was promoted to the rank of Sergeant of Engineers, (which rank I held without ever being placed in arrest or even reprimanded), until March 1861, when through the instrumentality of Generals Scott, Fatten, Cullum and the Hon. Henry Wilson, I was appointed a 2nd Lieutenant of Artillery. Was detailed on the recruiting service as asst. mustering officer in Pennsylvania and Maryland until 1864, performing my duties to the satisfaction of my superior officers when ordered to join my Battery ("B" 2nd U.S. Arty.) in front of Richmond. Was in command of the Battery during the campaign of General Sheridan in the Shenandoah Valley, taking part in several battles. Promoted to the rank of Captain, June 11, 1864 and joined my present battery in March 1865 and accompanied the regiment to San Francisco, California, having been since stationed in the harbor to San Francisco, Cal, Fort Humboldt, Cal and in command of Fort Steilacoom, Washington Territory and, until recently, in command of Fort Tongass, Alaska Territory.

Since I have been an officer, I can say conscientiously that I have never neglected my duties intentionally in any way whatsoever. The administration of the affairs of my Battery have been such that I have had a less number of men Court Marshaled, less occasion for it and a less number of desertions than any company in the Army for the same period. Stationed within such easy access of British Columbia (less than eight miles) what other company commanders can say that they had no desertions in twenty months, this command on two occasions having received six month's [back] pay.

Having been in the service so long a time, I am incapacitated for any other profession in life and pray that my punishment may be such, if possible, that I alone may be the sufferer and not the innocent ones dependent on me for support.

I am, Sir

Very Respectfully
Your Obedient Servant

C. H. Peirce
Cap't, 2nd Reg. Arty.

---

* There does not seem to be record that the president responded to Captain Peirce however, the letter may have been considered when Peirce was appointed lighthouse keeper. Here was obviously a man of good discipline who had spent his working years in government and was untrained for any gainful employment outside the government service. —Editor

Appendix C
Peirce Family Reunion at Historic Lighthouse

Under a sunny sky in the shadow of the Yaquina Bay Lighthouse, four generations of the descendants of Charles and Sarah Peirce met, many for the first time, on October 7, 1991.

Captain Charles Peirce was the only keeper of the lighthouse because the lighthouse operated only three years.

The range of ages represented at this unique yard party were from 84-year old Agnes Daniels, Depoe Bay, to Alex Hyde, 3, Portland.

The day was spent eating, getting acquainted, ooking at and identifying family photographs and visiting the lighthouse.

The event was featured in the *Gazette-Times,* Corvallis (Oct. 8), and in the *News Times* Newport (Oct. 16).

The roster here is transcribed from the Guest Register circulated at the reunion. The editor trusts the spellings are correct as the names appear in a variety of styles of penmanship.

Collum McLean, Depoe Bay, Ore.
Andrew Store, Coupeville, Wash.
Dorothy Hamilton, Twin Falls, Ida.
Melissa Davison, Hansen, Ida.
John Charles Goodman, Anchorage, Als.
Terri Shelby, Albany, Ore.
Jeanne Goodman Dyer, Silverdale, Wash.
Patrick Goodman, Anchorage, Als.
Rosalie Belcher, Bandon, Ore.
Mike Shelby, Albany, Ore.
Pat Moynahan, Morton, Wash.
Agnes Daniels, Depoe Bay, Ore.
Carol Dawn Eveleth, Hasden, Ida.
Michael Evelith. Hansen, Ida.
Nora McClain, Albany, Ore.
Gary McClain, Albany, Ore.
Megan M. Hyde, Portland, Ore.

Joe A. Hyde, Portland, Ore.
Alex Hyde, Portland, Ore.
Marty Hyde, Portland, Ore.
Barbara McLean, Seattle, Wash.
Bruce McLean, Seattle, Wash.
Phoebe McClain, Albany, Ore.
Robert S. McClain, Albany, Ore.
Phillip McLain, Seattle, Wash.
Johanna McLain, Seattle, Wash.
Linda Belcher, Bandon, Ore.
Michael Becker, Bandon, Ore.
Melinda McLean Stone, Coupeville, Wash.
Ian Stone, Coupeville, Wash
Robert M. Shelby, Albany, Ore.
Pete Shelby, Albany, Ore.
Jennifer McLean, Seattle, Wash.
Thomas Sanders, Seattle, Wash.

Bibliography

Evans, James R. *Flagstaff Hill on the National Historic Oregon Trail*. Webb Research Group. 1992.

Gibbs, James A. *Oregon's Salty Coast*. Webb Research Group. 1994.

_____. *Oregon's Seacoast Lighthouses*. Webb Research Group. 1992.

Gilkey, Helen M. *A Spring Flora of Northwestern Oregon*. private print. 1929.

Helbock, Richard. *Oregon Post Offices 1847-1982* LaPosta. 1982.

King, Frank. "Tidepool nature's backdoor," in *Statesman Journal* Salem, Ore. Sept. 30, 1993 p. C-1.

Light List, Pacific Coast. U.S. Dept. of Commerce. Lighthouse Service. 1934.

Light List, Pacific Coast and Pacific Islands. Dept. of Transportation. US Gov Print Office. 1982.

Mershon, Helen M. "Fate of 'Old Ghost Hangs'" in *Oregon Journal* Oct 28, 1964.

Nokes, J. Richard. *Columbia's River; the Voyages of Robert Gray, 1787-1793*. Wash. State Hist. Soc. 1991.

Oregon: End of the Trail. Federal Writers Project. WPA. Binford and Mort. 1940.

Trees, The Yearbook of Agriculture - 1949. U. S. Dept. of Agriculture. Gov. Print. Office. 1949.

United States Coast Pilot No. 7: Pacific Coast. U.S. Dept of Commerce NOAA. US Gov Print Office. 1983.

Webber, Bert. *Indians Along the Oregon Trail*. (Expanded Ed.) Webb Research Group. 1992.

_____. *Silent Siege-III: Japanese Attacks on North America in World War II, Ships Sunk, Air Raids, Bombs Dropped, Civilians Killed (Documentary)*. Webb Research Group. 1992.

Webber, Bert and Margie Webber. *Bayocean; The Oregon Town That Fell into the Sea*. Webb Research Group. 1989.

_____. *Lakeport; Ghost Town of the South Oregon Coast*. Webb Research Group. 1990.

_____. *Terrible Tilly: Tillamook Rock Lighthouse; The Biography of a Lighthouse An Oregon Documentary*. Webb Research Group. 1992.

Illustration Credits

Front cover Dorothy Wall
- ii   Bert Webber collection (bwc)
- vi   Bert Webber
- 8   bwc
- 10   (top) bwc; (lower) Bert Webber
- 11   (top) Lincoln County Historical Society (LCHS); (lower) Bert Webber
- 12   Bert Webber
- 16-17   *Ency Britannica* 11th Ed
- 18   Shore Village Museum, Rockland, Maine
- 19   Dorothy Wall
- 22   Jim Gibbs collection
- 24   bwc
- 28   Dorothy Wall
- 29   Bert Webber
- 30   (top) James A. Gibbs collection (jagc); (center and lower) LCHS
- 32   LCHS
- 36-38   Dorothy Wall collection (dwc)
- 39   dwc
- 42-43   dwc
- 44   bwc
- 45   (left) bwc; (right) dwc
- 47   dwc
- 50   Top LCHS
- 52-53   (LCHS)
- 54   (top) LCHS; (lower) jagc
- 55   (top) bwc; (lower) (LCHS)
- 59   bwc
- 62   (LCHS)
- 63-65   dwc
- 68   dwc
- 70-71   dwc
- 78   dwc
- 82   Dorothy Wall
- 90   Bert Webber
- 93   Dorothy Wall
- 94-95   dwc
- 96-97   dwc
- 98   Bert Webber
- 100-101   Dorothy Wall
- 102-105   Bert Webber
- 106   (top) bwc; (lower) Bert Webber
- 107   bwc
- 108   jagc
- 110-111   Bert Webber
- 115   dwc

The Author

A recipient of a Governor's award for Volunteerism in 1992, retired and happy Dorothy Wall, and her husband Les, are Volunteer Hosts with the Oregon State Parks. She said, "we just sort of fell into this one – Yaquina Bay State Park – when we applied to the program in 1988."

Yaquina Bay Lighthouse was their first assignment then they were sent to various other parks but always found themselves back at the lighthouse where they enjoy the volunteer work the best.

Over the years, people brought in old documents, newspaper clippings, pictures and other bits of information about the lighthouse. After accumulating a box of these over several years, she began to think about organizing this collection into a book. One of her first steps was to take classes for writers at a community college.

Born in Salem, Oregon in the late 1920's, Dorothy recalls it was a happy time to spend a childhood. Many of her school chums were in World War II. Wanting to help the war effort, her first volunteer job was working in the Office of Price Administration (OPA). Here she helped people register for the ration stamps for many foods and other goods people had always taken for granted but on account of the war, were in short supply.

She was schooled in Salem though a 2-year junior college program. After marrying, she and her husband, of 44 years at this writing, moved to a rural area near Albany where they reared a family of four boys and now have three grandsons and one grand-daughter.

Dorothy Wall wrote the script for the video of the lighthouse produced by the Friends of Yaquina Bay Lighthouse. She and Les are both on the Board of the Friends and she edits the regular newsletter. This is her first book.

*   *   *

Bert Webber is a research photojournalist, editor and publisher. He has written and published a number of books on a wide variety of subjects primarily about Oregon and the Oregon Trail. He is listed in *Contemporary Authors* and in *Who's Who in the West*. For a list of Webber books, consult *Books in Print* which can be found in most public libraries and in many independent book stores. ◊

Index

Illustrations are indicated in **bold *italic*** page numbers

Personal Notes and Comments

Personal Notes and Comments

Personal Notes and Comments

Personal Notes and Comments

Personal Notes and Comments